Hogan's Heroes

TV Milestones

HOGAN'S HEROES

Robert R. Shandley

TV MILESTONES SERIES

Wayne State University Press, Detroit

15 14 13 12 11   5 4 3 2 1

Library of Congress Cataloging-in-Publication Data

Shandley, Robert R.
Hogan's heroes / Robert R. Shandley.
p. cm. — (TV milestones)
Includes bibliographical references and index.
ISBN 978-0-8143-3416-4 (pbk. : alk. paper)
1. Hogan's heroes (Television program) I. Title.
PN1992.77.H56S53 2011
791.45'7—dc22
2011006747

For Ann, John, Tom, Betty, Cathy, and Janet

CONTENTS

ACKNOWLEDGMENTS   ix

Introduction   1

1. *Hogan's Heroes* and the Late 1960s America   19

2. Removing the History from World War II   47

3. *Hogan's Heroes* and Generational Change   75

Conclusion   103

NOTES   105

FILMOGRAPHY   111

INDEX   115

vii

Even small volumes need friends and this one has had a few. Texas A&M University has provided me with an institutional home, brilliant colleagues, and energetic students for fifteen years. The Melbern G. Glasscock Center for Humanities Research at Texas A&M University provided me an internal leave during which time I finished the first draft of this project and began another. The Department of European and Classical Languages and Cultures and the Film Studies Program have proven to be verdant fields of discussion and exchange.

I would like to thank the series editors, Barry Keith Grant and Jeannette Sloniowski, for supporting the project from the start. Annie Martin at Wayne State University Press has shown great patience in shepherding this project to completion. As always, my colleague Anne Morey has provided both intellectual support and critical feedback to my ideas.

My wife, Linda Radzik, is my first and best reader. She took particular pleasure in cutting large chunks of needless verbiage from the manuscript. I am glad to have offered her a place to take out her aggressions.

I am not sure I will ever have another project that our daughter, Mary, will appreciate as much as this one. She watched all 168 episodes of *Hogan's Heroes* with me, including multiple viewings of some of them. Somehow she has still become literate, talented, and intelligent, though the show certainly added to her goofiness.

My own siblings have been a far more important part of my life than they will ever realize. Whether well or poorly, they raised me. I watched my first episode of *Hogan's Heroes* in their company. Because of them I got to view age-inappropriate 1960s television shows such as *Laugh-In*, *The Smothers Brothers Comedy Hour*, and *Love, American Style*. More importantly, they did their best to look after me, keep me out of trouble, and challenge me. It is to them that I dedicate this book.

In the creative offices of Columbia Broadcasting System (CBS), the network that gave us a talking horse (*Mister Ed*, 1961–66), a stranded extraterrestrial (*My Favorite Martian*, 1963), and a beautiful domesticated robot (*My Living Doll*, 1964), it is not hard to imagine a show pitch like the following: "Hey, what if we did a comedy about a World War II German POW camp with a bunch of funny Nazis, where the prisoners are really in charge of the camp?" The network, which was leading the ratings in prime-time programming at the time, must have been rather certain of its ability to turn anything into comedy. And that confidence was well justified. *Hogan's Heroes* ran on CBS from September 1965 through April 1971. Set in World War II, the show presents a band of talented and irreverent prisoners of war who constantly outwit their German captors and use espionage and sabotage to thwart the Nazi war machine.

U.S. Air Force colonel Robert E. Hogan, the senior officer among the prisoners, operates a sabotage ring from the confines of Stalag 13, a camp run by toady Prussian officer Colonel Wilhelm Klink and his idiotic assistant, Sergeant Schultz. Hogan's band of coconspirators includes a mix of British, French, and American enlisted men. A series with a relatively large recurring cast, the show's regulars also include Klink's superior, General Burkhalter, Major Hochstetter of the Gestapo, and a set of Wagnerian blond-wigged secretaries. In generic terms, *Hogan's Heroes* is a mix of the military comedy and the spy thriller, a combination that would provide room for the series to stay ideologically relevant.

Moderately successful in its network run, remaining among the top twenty-five most highly rated programs for all six seasons, *Hogan's Heroes* has enjoyed constant play in syndicated rerelease since its cancellation by CBS. As I will argue in this book, *Hogan's Heroes* reveals the parameters of comedy about the absurdities of militarism and war in an age before American television embraced the conventions of comedic social realism that would define the more critically acclaimed *M*A*S*H*. Un-

Klink (Werner Klemperer), Schultz (John Banner), and Hogan (Bob Crane) in Stalag 13. ("Operation Briefcase," October 7, 1966)

like this latter series, *Hogan's Heroes* faced the challenge of satirizing war during the most uncertain period of the most controversial war in American history. The run of *Hogan's Heroes* corresponds with the crucial period of America's presence in Vietnam, from the escalation of hostilities in 1965 to the beginning of the American military withdrawal from Southeast Asia in the early 1970s. In an era in which attitudes about the military, patriotism, and authority were undergoing a sea change, *Hogan's Heroes'* response to those issues tells us much about the possibilities and limits of prime-time television to engage those changes.

To succeed the show had to speak to its moment, but the drive to put television properties into syndication for as long as possible also motivated the producers to avoid cultural references that were likely to feel outdated in a few years. It is in this conflicted effort to keep the show in the moment without necessarily appearing to be topical that I will be able to locate how *Hogan's Heroes* engages with its own historical context. *Hogan's Heroes'* ability to negotiate this difficult terrain during an incredibly tumultuous period in American history may well serve as its most important contribution to television history.

Negotiating the political currents of the mid- to late 1960s was difficult enough, but the setting of *Hogan's Heroes* required it to negotiate the past as well. The ridiculousness of the show's premise—namely, a cheery sitcom set in a World War II German POW camp—led to considerable critical discontent. In fact, it is hard to disagree with the show's detractors. The laugh track is the cuing device of almost all sitcoms of the era that assures the viewer that it is all right to laugh at what might otherwise be deemed inappropriate. In *Hogan's Heroes*, the real, horrific history of National Socialism and German military aggression has given way to a satire about something else, something about which it is acceptable to laugh. Perhaps the most consistent source of the series' humor was the presumed reverence with which the war had been treated to that point. CBS publicist

Stan Freberg's suggestion for a publicity campaign for the series addresses the full range of absurdity the network faced in fitting *Hogan's Heroes* into the moment: "If you liked World War II, you'll love *Hogan's Heroes*."[1] While it is unclear whether the tagline was ever used, it captures the confrontation of values that is at the heart of *Hogan's Heroes'* premise.

Method

The book is divided into three chapters. First I will place *Hogan's Heroes* within its generic and television history contexts. I will then place the series within the historical, filmic, and televisual discourses surrounding World War II. Finally I will demonstrate how the series uses its generic framework to engage in the debates about the conflict in Vietnam and American militarism.

Hogan's Heroes presents war as an unending series of small events rather than a steady progress to victory. Indeed contrary to the standard teleological history of World War II that necessarily culminates in an Allied victory, *Hogan's Heroes* offers a war filled with infinite recurrence. No matter how many times Hogan and his saboteurs destroy the Nazis' latest miracle weapon or munitions depot, subsequent missions will require them to do the same. Not unlike the helicopters that deliver the wounded in every episode of *M*A*S*H* (CBS, 1972–83), each episode of *Hogan's Heroes* presents an endless war with enduring obstacles, one that looks more like Walter Cronkite's description of the Vietnam conflict as "mired in a stalemate" than a certain march toward victory in the European theater of World War II.

While the book will argue for *Hogan's Heroes'* usefulness as a meter of attitudes regarding the Southeast Asian war, I would not want to overstate the case. *Hogan's Heroes'* importance lies in its function as a transition between the least-common-denominator programming of the early 1960s and the representation of much more modern lifestyles and political sensibilities that CBS introduced with shows such as *All in the Family* (1971–79), *The Mary Tyler Moore Show* (1970–77), *The Bob Newhart Show* (1972–78), and, of course, *M*A*S*H*, all of which eventually ran together in the CBS Saturday night lineup. Throughout most of the run of *Hogan's Heroes*, this segment of the audience was not interested in a direct confrontation of the Johnson administration's escalation of the Vietnam conflict. *Hogan's Heroes*, a series about another war, merely indicates the level of criticism that the era's audience was willing and capable of absorbing.

In interpreting television, one faces choices about the proper object of inquiry, the individual episodes, which the audience members would be expected to view in a single sitting, or the series as a whole, which, producers knew, had a constantly shifting audience. Viewers may start watching a series weeks or even whole seasons after it initially appears. They may not view the show every week. Given the standard pattern that began in earnest at CBS in 1967 in which a season of a series is run and then repeated before the next season begins, viewers are likely to see episodes out of their original order. Readers of books predictably start at chapter 1 and read linearly to the end of the book. This established convention means that authors can write later chapters presuming knowledge of everything that came earlier in the book. But for the producers of a television series, presuming such knowledge would function as a formula for discouraging potential audience members. So, television producers find themselves with conflicting motivations. They have reason to make each episode a freestanding product, comprehensible and meaningful on its own. But they also need to give the viewers of one episode a reason to tune in again the next week.

Now, well into the twenty-first century, television culture and television technologies have found ways of dealing with this tension. Viewers who have missed an episode or a season of a show can record the episodes on a digital video recorder, download the material they missed online, or buy a boxed set of the season. Fan blogs provide an even quicker way to catch up with a series. As Horace Newcomb has argued, since the 1980s, television producers have also developed a sophisticated form of storytelling, which he calls a "cumulative narrative."[2] He uses *Magnum P.I.* (CBS, 1980–88) as a prime example of a cumulative narrative model in which occasional viewers are able to understand single episodes while dedicated viewers are rewarded with subtle forms of information that provide increasingly nuanced understandings of characters and story lines.

Yet in the mid- to late 1960s, none of these technologies or narrative techniques for simultaneously addressing both new and dedicated viewers had been developed. The most frequently employed convention for drawing the viewer to the next week's installment was the two-part episode, which *Hogan's Heroes* used three times during its run. Indeed, apart from these rare sets, *Hogan's Heroes* employs very little continuity from one episode to the next. Characters who have met previously in the same season may or may not recognize one another. The series appears unaffected by the empirical timeline that the actual history of World War II might have imposed. *Hogan's Heroes* does not progress nor do the characters develop. The viewer will generally derive a similar amount of information whether she watches four episodes or forty. Thus, whether I am analyzing the performance style or ideological content, the episode is the primary unit of study for *Hogan's Heroes*. At this point in television history, a different strategy had to be used to connect with first-time viewers of the show and motivate dedicated viewing. As I will explore in more detail later in this chapter, *Hogan's Heroes* relied heavily on the conventions of the situation comedy genre. Indeed, *Hogan's Heroes* seems to revel in the strict rules it has set for its own narrative. Much of the fun of watching the show consists in seeing *how* the characters will come to the resolution that the viewer knows is guaranteed, and much of the humor is the comedy of repetition.

Interpreting *Hogan's Heroes*, then, is largely a matter of interpreting the generic structures that are instantiated in almost any episode in the set. However, my method will also include surveying a number of discrete episodes on a particular topic to elucidate what the series has to say about larger cultural and political issues. By noticing differences among these episodes over the run of the series, the reader will see how *Hogan's Heroes* responds to the shifting cultural, social, and political forces of the age.

The dominant description of the topography of American television in the mid-1960s stems from Newton Minow's 1961 speech to the National Association of Broadcasters in which he referred to the current television programming as a "vast wasteland . . . a procession of game shows, violence, audience participation shows, formula comedies about totally unbelievable families," and various other affronts to properly cultured taste.[3] While one might take Minow's speech as a bureaucratic affirmation of Max Horkheimer and T. W. Adorno's argument about the culture industry, his call for liberal reform, in which the media would eschew popular genres for more edifying content, is also haunted by the same kinds of cultural snobbery associated with critical theory. Neither Horkheimer and Adorno nor Commissioner Minow could imagine that even the most banal of mass culture products could engage critically in a manner no less articulate than the high art they advocated. In order to situate *Hogan's Heroes*' cultural voice, we must consider how it responded to a variety of generic trends both at CBS and the two other national networks.

CBS, which had dominated the prime-time hours with situation comedies for the previous three seasons, again won the 1963–64 ratings game with an increasing onslaught of rural comedies and variety shows. Even these shows could not keep global concerns from creeping into their small towns. In early 1964 more and more news about the turmoil in Indochina and American involvement in the region began to make its way into newscasts and onto the front pages of newspapers. By that summer, with passage of the Gulf of Tonkin Resolution, America was again preparing for war, and CBS found a way to narrate it. Gomer Pyle, the filling station attendant from their hit *The Andy Griffith Show* (1960–68), would join the marines and ready himself for combat.

Hogan's Heroes would become part of a genre of uniform comedies and dramas and television spy thrillers that occupied the network lineups in the early to mid-1960s and provided narrative backfill for Cold War tensions. The spy programs included shows such as *The Man from U.N.C.L.E.* (NBC, 1964–68), *Espionage* (NBC, 1963–64), *I Spy* (NBC, 1965–68), *Burke's Law* (ABC, 1963–66), *Mission: Impossible* (CBS, 1966–73), and the comedy *Get Smart* (NBC,1965–69; CBS, 1969–70). Starting in 1962, military sitcoms and dramas such as ABC's *McHale's Navy* (1962–66) and *Combat!* began occupying slots in the schedule. *Gomer Pyle, U.S.M.C.* (1964–69) was added to CBS's schedule in 1964. ABC kept up its quotient of military-related shows with the introduction that same season of *Twelve O'Clock High* (1964–67). By 1965, with the addition of *Hogan's Heroes*, which ran just before *Gomer Pyle, U.S.M.C.* on Friday nights; NBC's *The Wackiest Ship in the Army* (1965–66) and *Convoy* (1965); and ABC's *F Troop* (1965–67), uniform comedies and dramas occupied a dominant portion of the prime-time schedule. Both *Gomer Pyle, U.S.M.C.* and *Hogan's Heroes* made it into the top ten in Nielsen ratings that season, with *The Man from U.N.C.L.E.* and *Get Smart* cracking the top twenty. In the first year of the escalated American engagement in Vietnam, the spy and military genres were indeed a growing force in the prime-time schedule.

Erik Barnouw comments that "a visitor from another planet watching United States television for a week during the Vietnam escalation period might have concluded that viewers were being brainwashed by a cunning conspiracy determined to harness the nation—with special attention to its young—for war."[4] This description of the television schedule and the toy-marketing efforts in the fall of 1965 suggest that a unified propaganda force was preparing the United States for its escalating military involvement in Vietnam, although Barnouw intends simply an ironic description of the heavy network dependence on established television formulas. Still, the lineups of the three major American networks during this period, at least on their face, provide almost exaggerated animation of the critical theorists' claims about the deceptive quality of the products of the culture industry.[5] Militarism and espionage, they might argue, are presented as harmless and comedic, thereby dulling our perceptions of the horrors of war. But the simple premises of these shows alone do not reveal their capacity to offer critical perspectives on the military or the larger issues of the day, as I will argue at length with respect to *Hogan's Heroes*.

While it is hard to imagine that the overwhelming numbers of military and spy programs in this period could be unconnected to the political issues of the day, Barnouw is also right to point out that these programming choices are evidence that the networks, during this second decade of the age of television, relied heavily on established genres. Already in the late 1950s, CBS attracted large audiences with *The Phil Silvers Show* (1955–59), which featured Silvers's iconic Sergeant Bilko. The sitcom was situated in an army base in Kansas, where Bilko constantly concocts get-rich-quick schemes that often included swindling his own men. Episodes generally center on Bilko's newest plan in which his underlings readily participate. His designs often come at a cost to his commanding officer, Colonel Hall, who frets constantly about his inability to control Bilko.

The Phil Silvers Show pioneered the television military sitcom. It was successful throughout its entire four-year run. It set up the idea of the army squad as a family-like unit with the paternal, if not always reliable, sergeant at the lead. That formula, with occasional upgrades in rank, carries over to subsequent military comedies. Moreover, *The Phil Silvers Show* began the televisual portrayal of the military as a prankster fraternity rather than a mission-bound fighting unit. In *The Phil Silvers Show*, CBS had found a formula of forced solidarity that they would exploit in future series, including *Gomer Pyle, U.S.M.C.* and *Hogan's Heroes*.

The most successful of the uniform comedies, *Gomer Pyle*, pitted the dim-witted country boy, Pyle, against the angry Korean War vet, Sergeant Carter. The show uses the trope of the wise village idiot to reveal the self-righteousness of 1950s American conservatism as it is embodied in the sergeant. Carter is a remnant of the Eisenhower years, a drill instructor who harkens back to the heroic exploits of World War II without having directly participated in them.

Carter's apoplexy regarding Pyle's simpleminded charm is tamed by his own ambitions, since his reputation as a drill instructor and officer hinges on Pyle's behavior. If the humor derives from the combustive relationship between the two, many of the plots circulate around a shared desire to outwit the commissioned officer class as well as Carter's occasional recognition of Pyle's native moral intelligence. Thus, although Pyle is essentially held captive by Carter, their relationship functions as an almost pure example of Hegel's master/slave dialectic in which it is the former who remains dependent on the latter. In almost every episode Carter finds himself in need of Pyle's help, cooperation, or success. When, after the first season, *Hogan's Heroes* joined *Gomer Pyle* on CBS's Friday evening lineup, the dialectical formula would be taken even further. The Allied prisoners in *Hogan's Heroes* would soon prove invaluable to the welfare of their German captors, Colonel Klink and Sergeant Schultz.

While *Gomer Pyle, U.S.M.C.* provided *Hogan's Heroes* with a model for plot structure in the immediate CBS lineup, NBC's *The Man from U.N.C.L.E.* offered another important part of its narrative mix. Premiering in 1964 on Tuesday night, *The Man from U.N.C.L.E.* was an Ian Fleming project meant to take advantage of the success of the first James Bond film, *From Russia with Love* (Terence Young, 1963). Research showed that audiences liked the mixture of adventure and comedy.[6] In fact, NBC was putting together a prisoner of war comedy to couple with its success with *The Man from U.N.C.L.E. Campo 44* was to be set in an Italian POW camp. According to a fan book about *Hogan's Heroes*, when its creators, Albert Ruddy and Bernie Fein, caught wind of this development, they quickly set to work to pen a version of this scenario themselves.[7] Of course the other model for *Hogan's Heroes* was Billy Wilder's acclaimed 1953 POW film, *Stalag 17*, from which Ruddy and Fein obviously drew considerable material.

Ruddy and Fein apparently pitched the story first to NBC executives before turning to CBS.[8] Once receiving the green light, Ruddy and Fein sold the idea to CBS, which passed it on to Bing Crosby Productions to develop as a series. Hence CBS would add a show to its fall schedule in 1965 that would dovetail well with *Gomer Pyle, U.S.M.C.* and compete well (eventually directly) with *The Man from U.N.C.L.E.* All of these programs seemed, at first glance, to adhere strictly to the pro-military line of the networks in the mid-1960s.

In his book on television and the Cold War, J. Fred Mac-Donald describes the major networks as negligent of, if not complicit in, the escalating U.S. involvement in Vietnam. If television news had failed to make real to its audience the consequences of American involvement in Indochina, military sitcoms, MacDonald argues, exacerbated the problem. "These war stories and comedic encounters prolonged the inability of the American citizenry to confront the reality of war. Television showed the stylized armed conflict in which virile Yank soldiers triumphed in the end and comedic farce stripped war of its brutal, violent, murderous nature."[9] MacDonald's argument that the militarization of primetime normalized the notion of a larger military mobilization is credible. But, as I shall point out throughout my discussion of *Hogan's Heroes*, the medium's ability to both reflect and influence societal attitudes suggests that it did not always remain on the same side of any particular political or social issue. Indeed, one of the basic tenets of the study of popular culture is the assumed conversation that occurs between a particular cultural product and its audience. Thus, I would hypothesize that as audience attitudes shift, we will also see a shift in the television series' narrative attitude. To better understand the role of seemingly innocuous programs such as *Gomer Pyle*, *McHale's Navy*, or *Hogan's Heroes* in political discourse, I will first turn to the networks' presumption of who the potential audience was and how that changed over the run of the series.

The Audience of 1960s Television

The notion that U.S. networks first began to pursue particular demographic groups through programming in 1970 persists as one of the great myths of American television history. What was to become known as CBS's 1971 barnyard purge in which hits of the previous decade such as *The Beverly Hillbillies* (1962–71), *Mayberry R.F.D.* (1968–71), *Petticoat Junction* (1963–70), *Green Acres* (1965–71), *Gomer Pyle*, *Hee Haw* (CBS, 1969–71; produced and syndicated by Gaylord Productions, 1971–93), and *Hogan's Heroes* were removed from the schedule has come to be seen as the network's discovery of the need to pitch its programming to a higher income bracket rather than to a mass audience. There can be little doubt that such was indeed CBS's motivation. But, as Mark Alvey has argued, all three networks were already well aware of the notion of "quality demographics" in the 1950s.[10] Alvey goes on to show how the networks, specifically NBC and CBS, used demographic data selectively, when their mass ratings were down.

We do not need ratings data to ascertain to whom *Hogan's Heroes*, at least initially, was being pitched. Instead we can look to some of the early decisions that CBS made regarding the show. Early in 1965, CBS was making incremental gestures toward broader programming in color. A national survey of women in December 1964 showed that owners of color sets were more affluent, better educated, and more urban than the population as a whole.[11] *Hogan's Heroes* was one of the earliest shows on which CBS committed to color. Later in 1965, once it became clear that the production and sale of color sets were booming, CBS expanded its color offerings radically. Yet the fact that *Hogan's Heroes* made the earlier list is suggestive of its intended demographic appeal. My argument is that the shift in programming strategies from the 1960s to the 1970s does not turn on the sudden interest in demographics but instead on a shift in the strategies CBS used to reach the demographic it had been interested in for some time. When *Hogan's Heroes* was first broadcast, CBS aimed to attract its desired viewers through the technical innovation of color broadcasting. With the barnyard purge of 1971 the network's marketing efforts were refocused on the narrative and aesthetic qualities of the television shows it aired.

Why do CBS's original intentions for the series matter? It is because they bring us directly to a cluster of dichotomies around which our current understanding of American television history is organized, of which the tension between mass and demographic programming is the most obvious. The nature of the intended audience connects directly to the dichotomy between the understanding of 1960s television in "vast wasteland" terms and the critical acclaim shed on the 1970s products of MTM Enterprises and Norman Lear. This tension between 1960s and 1970s television rests precariously on a low art/high art distinction. Curiously enough, this distinction slips into television criticism at exactly the same moment that it undergoes forceful critique in literary and philosophical circles as classist and monolithic. The alleged low art/high art distinction becomes obvious in the critical reception of *Hogan Heroes*. For example, in a *New York Times* review of Mel Brooks's *The Producers* (1968), a film that also offered comic send-ups of Nazis, Renata Adler referred to *Hogan's Heroes* as "brute vulgarism."[12] For her it was part of a trend of debasement that she perceived throughout the cultural landscape.

This evaluation of *Hogan's Heroes* finds a striking contrast a few years later in the reception of *M*A*S*H*. Because of their tremendous range of shared characteristics, *M*A*S*H*, which premiered almost two years after *Hogan's Heroes* left the primetime schedule, can serve as a generic comparison. *M*A*S*H* offers an excellent example of CBS's attempt to reach a wealthier, more urban, more educated audience in the post-Vietnam era. Yet *Hogan's Heroes* is its precursor, as a military comedy that attempts broad appeal while working to keep its humor socially relevant enough to be effective. Much of the scholarly work on *M*A*S*H* starts with the assumption that the sitcom trials and tribulations of the medical unit during the Korean War is in fact a thinly veiled commentary on the Vietnam War. As such it is also generally regarded to be a televisual form of high art, in contrast to shows such as *Hogan's Heroes*.

In making his case for why *M*A*S*H* is television's "first dark comedy," David Scott Diffrient insists that "no other military focused sitcom—not *McHale's Navy* (ABC, 1962–66), not *McKeever and the Colonel* (NBC, 1962–63), not *Gomer Pyle, U.S.M.C.* (CBS, 1964–69), and not *Hogan's Heroes* (CBS, 1965–71)—was as satiric as *M*A*S*H*."[13] The combined politically critical and aesthetic merits of *M*A*S*H* have—legitimately—earned its place in television history. However, I would argue that Diffrient's comparison reflects both a lack of engagement with *Hogan's Heroes* (and, for that matter, the other series mentioned) and a failure to appreciate the greatest difference between the two series. Premiering on September 17, 1972, *M*A*S*H* had the benefit of conducting its treatment of the Vietnam War at a time when a vast consensus had emerged that shared its antiwar sentiments. *Hogan's Heroes*, as this study will reveal, is an artifact of the uncertainties and tumult of its era. *M*A*S*H* offers a humorous and elegiac treatment of the futility of war, while *Hogan's Heroes* produces running satirical commentary on the Vietnam War at its peak. Whether one prefers one series over the other does not negate the fact that an overdependence on satire was the most consistent critique of *Hogan's Heroes* both during and after its six-year network run. While it might be conceded that *Hogan's Heroes* offered a more restricted array of aesthetic forms than many of its successors, the series still registers a compelling engagement and occasional disruption in the social equilibrium of the time.

Before continuing, I should address a possible objection—namely, that I am putting up a relatively weak straw man regarding the perception of *Hogan's Heroes* as socially unengaged. Essentially this perception has been implied by what followed the series. That is to say, because what came after the "barnyard purge" constituted among critics and historians the prototype of "quality television," the purged shows are necessarily not quality. The latter are then categorically excluded from the reception ritual that Jane Feuer has attributed to the MTM Enterprises productions. "In interpreting an MTM programme, as a quality programme, the quality audience is permitted to enjoy a form of television which is seen as more literate, more stylistically complex, and more psychologically 'deep' than ordinary television fare."[14] Through justifying a normative aesthetic structure, Feuer wants to claim that the "quality" of the television show is inherent to the product. That is to say, she does not consider that one show is qualitatively better than another only if one applies one's own predetermined notions of quality.

Hogan's Heroes and the Sitcom as Genre

The question remains, If I cannot use aesthetic normativity as a starting point for a discussion of a television series, to what might I turn? What is it that makes *Hogan's Heroes* a compelling object of study forty years after it ended its network run? Rather than treat the series as exceptional, I will demonstrate how *Hogan's Heroes* functioned almost entirely within the conventions of the American television situation comedy. I will contend that those conventions not only make room for socially relevant comic narrative, they depend on such mode of address. The presumed harmlessness of sitcom banter allows a level of commentary that had proven difficult in any other arena of prime-time television.

Paul Attallah first made such claims about situation comedy decades ago in his article "The Unworthy Discourse."[15] He sets out to describe the constitutive elements of the sitcom as a genre. His description is worth quoting at length, because it provides a theoretical structure that will allow us to situate *Hogan's Heroes* in the discursive field of its moment. Attallah claims that a set of elements as well as their repetition creates the discourse of the sitcom:

1. The same tropes reappear. This can be something as banal as the physical appearance of the characters, the necessity of a funny look or gesture.
2. The same ways of setting up arguments or points to be resolved recur.
3. The same mode of address (wit) recurs.
4. The same way of imagining a situation that will be both funny and significant recurs; hence the necessity of establishing a homeostatic situation with well-defined, nonevolving main characters who nonetheless encounter an endless stream of minor, outside characters.
5. The same relationship between the product (sitcom)

and the institution (television) recurs; the various products must all achieve the same goal; hence the same mode of address.

6. The same relationship between the product and the empirical reality it is said to represent recurs. The same theory of representation is at work in all sitcoms; the way reality is thought to look and operate is heavily coded into every aspect of the representation, from the construction of narrative space to the definition of character types.

7. Ultimately the same conception of audience recurs. The discourse of the institution of television, which, like all discourses, is intended for someone, systematically arranges, orchestrates, and constitutes its audience through its construction of representation.[16]

Although Attallah overstates somewhat the determinative power of television genre discourse, his description reveals the many layers on which sitcoms make meaning. As I go through what *Hogan's Heroes* was and what it did, I will, at the same time, ask how it engaged its institutional setting.

When Attallah asserts that the sitcom rests "upon the encounter of dissonant or incompatible discursive hierarchies,"[17] he indicates something similar to what Kaja Silverman refers to as a challenge to the "dominant fiction."[18] In the mid-1960s, the incompatible discursive hierarchies or dominant fictions regarding American social and cultural unity were on the verge of collapse. *Hogan's Heroes* registers that collapse and offers a commentary that at the time was both legible and opaque enough to allow the show to be entertaining long after the issues of the day had changed.

Hogan's Heroes and
the Late 1960s America

*H*ogan's Heroes premiered in CBS's Friday night lineup on September 17, 1965, with the pilot episode, "The In-former." The pilot differed from the rest of the run in a number of significant ways. The pilot episode was shot in black and white.[1] Of course, the pilot episode is also what was used to sell the network on developing the show. Therefore it is not difficult to appreciate it as a primer for all parties as to how the series, its characters, its premise, and its audience will be conceived and addressed. Arguably, the pilot episode pushes the absurdities of the series' premise much further than any of the 167 subsequent episodes.

The opening credits of "The Informer" include the dateline "Germany, 1942." Lest the viewer suspect anything serious from the show, the opening martial percussion immediately shifts to the series' much more lighthearted theme song. *Hogan's Heroes* reveals the discursive cards with which it will play by introducing the combination of trappings of the German war machine and the comedic soundtrack. Once the credits introduce the main players, Sergeant Schultz is shown performing what will become his usual prisoner count, which falls short. A prisoner is missing, and Schultz appeals to Hogan for help. The prisoners stall the count until a replacement prisoner shows up. In case the dissonance has gone unnoticed, within ten seconds of the disappearance of the credits, the laugh track is employed for the first time. The rest of the episode must then concentrate on establishing what is so laughable about this situation and which social codes are going to be confronted. None of these confrontations can be set up without the primary conceit of the series—namely, that the Nazi Germans are buffoons on whose bodies most of the humor will be played out.

Minutes into the episode, the unruly group of prisoners distract the slow-witted Sergeant Schultz so a prisoner can escape under the fence. At that point the pilot episode also establishes the conceit that assures mutual cooperation between Schultz and the prisoners. The sergeant of the guard's fear that an escape would land him in trouble with his superiors motivates him, not only to turn a blind eye and a deaf ear to the prisoners' activities, but also to turn to them in times of need. The conceit disrupts the hegemonic understanding of military service that presumes that all uniformed service personnel are ideologically committed to the wars into which they are sent.

Shortly after introducing Schultz, the episode calls on two separate plotlines rooted in film history to anchor itself in a narrative tradition. The first is a plot by the camp officials to place a spy among the prisoners. This story line is drawn directly from Billy Wilder's 1953 film *Stalag 17*. The second is the perceived officer solidarity between Colonels Hogan and Klink. This trope, common to many combat films, was animated most thoroughly in Jean Renoir's canonical antiwar POW film, *The Grand Illusion* (1937). *Hogan's Heroes* exploits this narrative device in order to allow Hogan to evade Klink's attempts to control the prisoners and to find cover for own his sabotage plans. Because of their shared stripes and Hogan's status as senior POW officer, he has constant access to Klink's office and to Klink's psyche. Almost every one of the subsequent 167 episodes will depend on Klink's trust in and dependency on Hogan. The humor comes in each episode as Hogan abuses this trust.

The rest of the episode is organized around revealing the range of gimmicks and tools with which the prisoners will thwart the Nazi war machine, each of which draws its own laugh track. These include a coffeepot phone-tapping system, a watchdog delivery vehicle used as a smuggling device, a tunnel underneath the doghouse, and a flagpole displaying the Nazi banner but serving as a radio antenna for the prisoners. The episode also introduces the frequently employed brief sequence of Sergeant Kinchloe making contact with a British submarine (which is obviously a toy vessel in a bathtub).

The narrative of "The Informer" offers a corrective to Wilder's much bleaker *Stalag 17*. Here Hogan's gang is fully aware

From left: LeBeau (Robert Clary), Hogan, Kinchloe (Ivan Dixon), Carter (Larry Hovis), and Newkirk (Richard Dawson) listen in on Klink's office through a rigged coffeepot. ("Evening of the Generals," December 2, 1967)

that the newly arrived prisoner is a German spy. Rather than snuff him out, Hogan and company present their entire operation to him. The punch line of the episode rests on the impossibility of Hogan's operation, which, for the benefit of the spy, includes a blackmarket industry in military souvenirs and an underground spa for the prisoners. The POWs do not get caught because the idea of running a vast underground espionage and sabotage operation from inside a POW camp is too absurd for the German officers to believe.

Perhaps the biggest difference between the pilot and the subsequent series lies in the makeup of the dramatis personae. In "The Informer" actor Larry Hovis appears as a lieutenant trying to escape but is recast as Sergeant Andrew Carter from the next episode onward. More significantly, the key group of saboteurs includes Americans Hogan (Bob Crane) and Kinchloe (Ivan Dixon); the Frenchman, LeBeau (Robert Clary); and the Brit, Newkirk (Richard Dawson), but it also rounds out the Allied powers by including a Russian, Vladimir Minsk (Leonid Kinsky). Brenda Scott Royce offers Kinsky's reason for backing out of the series: "The moment we had a dress rehearsal and I saw German SS uniforms something very ugly rose in me. I visualized millions upon millions of bodies of innocent people murdered by the Nazis. One can hardly, in good taste, joke about it."[2] Kinsky's criticism would be one shared by dozens of critics over the course of the show's six-year run.

In effect, the pilot episode and opening sequence of *Hogan's Heroes* must establish the series, the premise of which appears markedly absurd, as a sitcom. Because its setting disrupts the narrative equilibrium of television comedy, the pilot episode and arguably the series become even more strictly bound to the generic codes Attallah identifies. A crucial aspect of the series that is introduced in "The Informer" is the deployment of the laugh track. If *Wikipedia* can be believed, a version of the pilot episode was screened for a preview audience without the laugh track and failed miserably.[3] As the episode now stands, the laugh track instructs the viewer to laugh at the various ways in which the prisoners dupe the guards. In some cases, as when a prisoner escapes underneath the fence or when Schultz enters the scene, the laugh track ensures comic relief rather than narrative tension. Although it remains doubtful that many would have been tempted to do so, the laugh track dissuades viewers from understanding the series as a spy thriller or drama.

As ranking officer among the prisoners, Colonel Robert Hogan functions as the paterfamilias of the entire ensemble. His sabotage and insurgency operation depends on a combination of his charm, quick wit, and good luck. Not only do the members of his band of marauders depend on him, so too do the camp commandant and sergeant of the guard, Klink and Schultz. Many episodes include a plot or subplot in which Schultz and/or Klink would be transferred to the Russian front if not for Hogan's trickery. As patriarch, Hogan is also entitled to the affections of almost any woman who crosses his path, especially if she is attached to a German officer. And, in almost every episode, the success of the mission at hand depends on an epiphany that will come to Hogan, one that is often signaled just before, and revealed just after, a commercial break.[4]

Hogan's counterpart and foil, Colonel Wilhelm Klink, is a pompous Prussian living with delusions of grandeur in a failed military career. If the audience sympathizes with him, it is only because he is a dim-witted and harmless loser. His ego is easily turned against him and almost every episode includes his falling victim to the pranks of the prisoners. Each story ends either with his frustration that something has been pulled over on him that he does not fully understand or his delusional happiness that he has thwarted the German war machinery from punishing his incompetence. Werner Klemperer plays him as effete and without the slightest trace of military demeanor.

Perhaps the most adorable and innocent character in the show is Sergeant Schultz. Portrayed as more of a house pet than a human, Schultz's loyalties can be rented upon the provision

Hogan always gets the girl, including Klink's secretary, Hilda (Sigrid Valdis). ("The Battle of Stalag 13," October 14, 1966)

of either treats or protection. Sometimes he is shown as being shocked or dismayed by the heroes' activities; other times he simply worries that they will get caught and he will suffer repercussions. No matter the circumstance, John Banner portrays the character as a quintessential "Schweik," the legendary imbecilic Austro-Hungarian soldier from World War I.[5] Unlike Klink, Schultz is rarely the target of the prisoners' sadistic humor; rather he is usually incorporated in their schemes. From the pilot episode onward, the viewer understands his stakes in cooperating with all sides. He is trying to avoid being sent into combat, especially at the Russian front. Hence, most of his discoveries are promptly followed by his famous quote: "I know nothing. I see nothing." Upon receiving this reassurance (or simply taking it for granted), the prisoners carry on with their plotting.

Hogan's Heroes balanced a large ensemble cast for six seasons, a considerable feat given the individual talents of the cast members. The show was able to sustain the cast with few changes for the entire run. The two major changes came after the first season and before the last. After one season of playing Klink's secretary, Helga, Cynthia Lynn was replaced by Crane's future wife, Sigrid Valdis, who played Hilda. Lynn, who continued to appear occasionally in the series in other roles, was apparently switched out to increase the sexual spark between Hogan and the secretary. This substitution was initially a response to the sexual repartee in NBC's *The Man from U.N.C.L.E.* with which *Hogan's Heroes* was in direct ratings competition in the second season.[6]

The more significant change to the ensemble came at the end of the fifth season. Ivan Dixon, who played the troop's communication specialist, Sergeant Kinchloe (referred to throughout the series as "Kinch"), left the show to pursue a career in directing. Dixon had been a part of a mid-1960s attempt by CBS and NBC to include more African Americans in the primetime mainstream. Bill Cosby starred in *I Spy* from 1965 to 1968, while Greg Morris played the part of Barney Collier in *Mission: Impossible* from 1966 to 1973. In all three cases, the characters played by the black actors were equal or superior to their white counterparts in terms of rank and intellectual resources. In the case of *Hogan's Heroes*, this meant that Dixon generally played Kinch as the straight man and confidant to Colonel Hogan rather than engaging in the zany shenanigans of the other prisoners. Kinch is the one person on either side of the war to whom Hogan does not condescend. While this made the character respectable, it often caused him to disappear among the comedic actions of the other members of the ensemble. When Dixon left the show in 1970, he was replaced by Kenneth Washington, who played Sergeant Richard Baker, another African American straight man. The show never endeavored to explain what happened to Kinch.

Apart from those two instances, however, the ensemble remained intact for all six seasons. The rest of the regulars included the dueling duo of Corporals Louis LeBeau and Peter Newkirk, played by Robert Clary and Richard Dawson respectively. The two cooperate on missions while playing out French and British clichés and rivalries. Hovis's Sergeant Carter embodies the contradiction of being both the intellectual counterpart to Schultz and a munitions expert. While *Hogan's Heroes* depicts the prisoners in constant squabble with one another, they also maintain an unspoken solidarity akin to that seen most often in other male genres, such as combat and cop/buddy films.

Hogan's Heroes developed another rivalry that would continue throughout the last half of the series' run. Klink's direct commander is General Burkhalter, played by Leon Askin. From the beginning, Burkhalter is a target of the prisoners' pranks and subversions. It is Burkhalter who utters the constant threat to send Klink to the Russian front. In one of the series' few nods to actual history, the second season introduces the Gestapo major Hochstetter, played by Howard Caine. Initially, Burkhalter and Hochstetter were interchangeable figures, both serving as authoritarian threats to Klink. Royce notes that "when Leon Askin was working in Europe and was unavailable for filming, all the scripts featuring Burkhalter were changed to Hochstetter."[7] It was not until late in the third season that the two appeared together in an episode. In numerous episodes thereafter these two characters play out the rivalry between the German military and the Nazi paramilitary organizations, an institutional competition that has parallels in the historical record.

Attallah's rubric describes the basic plot rules around which each episode is organized. Colonel Klink brags in every episode that no one has ever escaped from Stalag 13.[8] This conceit trumps all others in the *Hogan's Heroes* story line, for it assures

Gestapo agent Hochstetter (Howard Caine) with the trappings of the Third Reich. The prisoners listen to the conversation through a secret microphone in the Hitler picture in the background. ("Fat Hermann, Go Home," January 16, 1970)

that, despite their incompetence, Klink and Schultz will continue their command of the camp. The prisoners are dependent on Klink's delusion of competence and Schultz's indifference to the outcome of the war to carry out their sabotage missions. Thus, not only must the camp stay open, but the current staff must also be retained. The POWs could have no guarantee that the next crew would be as reliably idiotic and gullible. This retention of the status quo is not just assumed, as in many sitcoms, rather it becomes a primary plot motivator of dozens of episodes.

If the German staff must remain in place, the same set of prisoners must necessarily also stay put. During the run of the series several episodes set up one of the core prisoners in a scenario in which he seeks to leave the camp for good, only to be brought back into the solidarity of the group. In "Request Permission to Escape" (April 29, 1966), Carter receives a "Dear John" letter from his girlfriend and hopes to return home to change her mind. In "Cuisine à la Stalag 13" (September 20, 1970), LeBeau is set to heed the call of General de Gaulle to join the Free French in England until he realizes that he is already playing a part in that fight from inside the prison camp. And in "Hogan, Go Home" (January 13, 1968), the colonel is moved to return to a hero's welcome in the States, only to decide that his mission in Germany is not yet finished. To be sure, the demands of the culture industry to maintain the set of characters to which the television audience had grown accustomed served as the primary extradiegetic reason why the viewer can be confident that, at the end of the episode, the characters will remain in the camp. Nevertheless, the implied diegetic threat in each episode is that the loss of the particular inmate will mean the end of the sabotage mission to which the prisoners are dedicated.

Regardless of the hopelessness of any given situation in *Hogan's Heroes*, another plot rule dictates that the Germans never succeed. At the end of the episode they must always come across as easily duped, corrupt, and doomed. Lore has it that Werner Klemperer based his acceptance of the role of Klink on the condition that the Germans' exploits never end in victory.[9] As Klemperer himself was forced into American exile upon Hitler's rise to power in 1933, this story holds some weight. Given the overall tone of the series and the rest of the show's diegetic parameters, however, it seems just as likely that such a stipulation by Klemperer would have been unnecessary. Quoted more directly, Klemperer explains his involvement in the show less drastically. He said that he agreed to play the part "as long as I can be sure to put him in the place he belongs. I wouldn't want to play Klink if he were a hero."[10] But more than simply easing Klemperer's historical sensibilities, the conceit that the

Germans never succeed maintains the disequilibrium necessary for the comedy to work. The antiauthoritarian pranksters depend on the helplessness of the German military brass to fuel their antics. The audience must buy into the idea that this is not a life-or-death situation, because the Germans will never succeed.

Hogan's Heroes and Narrative Consistency

A thorough viewing of all 168 episodes of *Hogan's Heroes*, both in and out of order, reveals a number of important traits of the series. Not only does each episode have next to nothing to do with the one that preceded it, the series suggests no particular temporal relationship at all among the episodes. That is to say, for a series that is set within an actual historical event—namely, World War II—and that often uses real moments in that war as plot devices around which to organize a particular episode, the series offers no overall story arc. The pilot episode places us in a particular time and place, "Germany, 1942." Episode 65, "D-Day at Stalag 13" (September 23, 1967), ran in the second season despite any number of scenarios in the preceding episodes in which Allies and Germans were already engaged in the post-D-day ground war. Moreover, episode 27, "The Safecracker Suite" (March 25, 1966), turns on the plot to assassinate Hitler, which occurred over a month after D-day. The relationship between *Hogan's Heroes* and the history and memory of World War II will warrant extended discussion in chapter 2. For now it is merely important to note that the historical march of time establishes no causal relationships among occurrences in the series. While the show occasionally gives a nod to real historical moments, these events occur in temporal isolation from one another. However, the series does manage to keep antagonists who have been blown up in previous episodes from returning to be blown up again.

Not only does history not develop, the characters remain equally frozen. This is, of course, in keeping with Attallah's description of genre television's need to establish homeostatic situations. Klink is every bit as gullible in the last episode of the series as he is in the first. The prisoners do not appear to have learned any new tactics from their previous exploits. Schultz neither becomes more resentful of the ways in which the prisoners trick and take advantage of him nor is he openly disturbed at the disrespect shown to him by Klink. Despite hundreds of misadventures, Burkhalter's reaction to Klink's incompetence never brings him to act on the threat of removing the latter to the Russian front. While numerous episodes begin with either Burkhalter or Hochstetter noticing that an unusual amount of sabotage has been occurring near the base, the show never portrays them in systematic pursuit of the cause. Just like the story lines, most character development is contained to the episode itself and never carries over to subsequent ones.

One revealing example of static characterization comes in the episode titled "War Takes a Holiday" (January27, 1968). This installment provides a prewar backstory for Klink and Schultz, something longtime viewers of the program may have wanted. Here the viewer is told that before the war Klink, despite his constant claims of aristocratic heritage and lifelong military service, served as a bookkeeper. Schultz, who has long suffered under the yoke of Klink's phony authority, was Germany's largest toy manufacturer. Due to Hogan's pranks, the Germans at Stalag 13 believe the war is coming to an end. This leads Klink, who has just discovered Schultz's background, to solicit postwar employment from his soon-to-be former underling. Had this storyline been developed from the start or had it been played on thereafter, it could have added a productive source of humor for subsequent episodes. However, the characters never again mention this background.

Many episodes involve a physical alteration to the camp, which by the next episode no longer appears. The most blatant of these occurs in episode 18, "The Gold Rush" (January 14, 1966), in which the prisoners scheme to retrieve gold bouillon stolen by the Nazis by disguising them as bricks. They then use the bricks to build a front stoop for Klink. The gold is meant to stay there until the camp is liberated at which time it would presumably be repatriated. But by the next episode the former wooden stoop returns to the set, with no recognition of the previous shenanigans. Another curious aspect of the series is the fact that characters who have met each other in previous episodes often evince no recognition of that history. Corporal Newkirk is often presented to Klink as having had backgrounds ranging from barrister to painter. This narrative amnesia contributes to the pool of available plot devices that the writers can use to construct an episode, most important for these purposes being plots that turn on misrecognition of some sort. The prisoners have a stockpile of German uniforms and civilian clothes that they wear to town or around the camp as needed.

Even more glaring are the number of recurring plotlines. Brenda Scott Royce has made an inventory of the repeats.[11] The most frequently used conceit is that the Germans have a new weapon that the prisoners must either photograph, destroy, or both. A variation of this theme is that a scientist comes to the camp who is developing such a weapon. He must invariably be either killed or kidnapped. Sabotage against nearby targets often motivates the prisoners, who set out to destroy a bridge, factory, or train. Each mission is described as impossible before Hogan's epiphany reveals to the saboteurs how it will all go down. The series also employs the frequent plot device in which either Klink or Schultz is in danger of being transferred to the Russian front or otherwise replaced. A number of episodes pattern themselves after the pilot in which a spy is planted in the camp in order to discover Hogan's subversions. About an equal number of episodes involve a high-ranking German officer who needs the prisoners' help in defecting. In short, the series cycles through a set of plotlines, all of which are established in the first season.

The writers return occasionally to certain narrative strands only to drop them again almost as quickly. One such recurrence surrounds Burkhalter's repeated attempts to get Klink to marry the general's widowed sister, which happens in five different episodes. Another concerns the exploits of the bungling British colonel Crittendon (a rank that did not actually exist in the Royal Air Force at the time). Crittendon outranks Hogan, having served longer in the rank of colonel, and therefore assumes command as senior POW whenever he lands in Stalag 13, often threatening the delicate missions with his comic misdeeds. The other character that recurs almost every season is Marya, the Russian spy with whom Hogan always collaborates unwillingly.

The heroes plot sabotage in their underground laboratory. ("Tanks for the Memory," November 11, 1966)

Her recurrence, which will be discussed in more detail in chapter 3, allows the series to include Cold War humor in its joke repertoire.

One might be tempted to ask how *Hogan's Heroes* managed to retain an audience given its predictable and largely static nature. That question, arguably, simply misses the point of genre television, especially in its 1960s form. The formula of the situation comedy of the era calls for the episode to set up a problem in the first five minutes, a problem that the remainder of the episode will be devoted to solving. The pleasure to the viewer is not only to be found in the eventual solution but also in the outlandishness of the setup. As with most formulaic narratives, any viewer enjoyment also involves how the episode finds resolution within the rules of that genre. The habitual viewer of *Hogan's Heroes* understands its particular rule set and enjoys seeing how the episode will move the plot back to eventual stasis. Thus she takes pleasure in a certain mastery of the narrative formula.[12]

Hogan's Heroes and Racial Politics

If one insists on the later development of story arcs and character development as sine qua non for television worthy of study, then *Hogan's Heroes* is certainly the wrong place to look. But, if we look to generic structure and the construction of the episodes themselves, the viewer will find material that can motivate critical work. In what follows I will demonstrate that the episode is the proper unit of analysis for understanding this series by reading three examples that place the character of Sergeant Kinchloe at the center of the action. The installments were scattered throughout the five years of the series in which Ivan Dixon played Kinch. While these episodes do not refer to one another in any way, they all circulate around questions of race, race relations, and racial stereotypes. Each episode opens itself up for a useful reading about how the series spoke to the highly charged civil rights issues of its time. These readings illustrate the ways in which the fantasy construct of *Hogan's Heroes* is open to the influences of the larger world. They also show how one can perform a cultural/historical analysis of a television series that organizes itself within the confines of a generic structure. The Kinch episodes reveal attitudes about American racial politics that reflect both the upheaval of the civil rights movement and American pop culture's difficulty in finding a voice to represent those politics.

One theme in the series, and in its predecessor *Stalag 17*, is that part of the hardship of a POW camp is the men's separation from female company. Humor is drawn from Hogan's ease in overcoming even this attempt by the Germans to control him. Whenever any attractive female appears in an episode the probability is high that Hogan will wind up in her embrace. Hogan's men are not so lucky. Juvenile expressions of sexuality on the part of the enlisted men and ill-fated antics designed to bring them close to women become a part of the standard comic repertoire of the show. However, Kinch remains exceptional on this score, usually keeping a dignified distance from such shenanigans. This might have been due to reluctance on the part of the writers to place an African American in a possible miscegenic situation that would have likely met with controversy among the 1960s viewing public. Thus, if Kinchloe was going to become a full member of the group, they would have to devise a scenario in which he too could pursue affection in the midst of war.

Such is the setup for episode 26, "The Prince from the Phone Company" (March 18, 1966). This episode is one of thirty-four installments directed by Gene Reynolds, who represents one of the primary continuities between *Hogan's Heroes* and *M*A*S*H*, of which he was a cocreator and executive producer. Reynolds's writing credits connect him even further to the more critically acclaimed shows of the 1970s, as he was credited as the creator of *Lou Grant*, the dramatic spin-off of *The Mary Tyler Moore Show*.[13]

The episode revolves around the prisoners' sudden need for a large amount of cash. This need coincides with a visit to the camp by the royal head of an unnamed African country, Prince Makabana (also played by Dixon), who has come to the Reich to negotiate port rights with the German navy. The prince's demeanor suggests a postcolonial dictator much more than it does wartime African royalty. Because of their resemblance, Kinchloe is conscripted to replace the prince. The plan to steal the German cash and set up a bombing of German submarines encounters a glitch when the prince's princess arrives at the camp. Although Princess Yawanda notices the switch, she initiates affections with Kinch, a romance ensues, and the mission succeeds without a hitch.

"The Prince from the Phone Company" touches gingerly on racial politics, despite the primacy of race in the script. At some point, the prince notes that he is not so inclined to cooperate with the Reich given the führer's comments about "his people." This comment subtly equates Nazi and American racial politics, actually recalling debates in the early World War II years among many leaders in the African American community. In a country in which lynching was still an unpunished public celebration in the South, African American leaders were rightfully concerned that Americans may not have had the moral high ground they needed when they entered the war. Though, as is the case with any potentially incendiary political speech during the first year of the series, the comments are passed over quickly enough so as not to draw attention and, like most other political commentary in the show, underscored with a laugh track. Princess Yawanda, who turns out to be from Cleveland, shows no reluctance in helping the Allied cause. It is noteworthy that this romance, unlike any of the others pursued by Hogan or his men, is treated seriously. The episode suggests a plausible affinity between Kinch and the princess, a serious connection that no other romantic interlude in the series ever broaches.

Both the prince's brief commentary and the princess's willingness to cooperate serve as an important baseline in our measurement of *Hogan's Heroes'* social engagement. For as the series progresses, so too do its politics. Of course, "The Prince from the Phone Company" portrays some rather conservative and indeed troubling attitudes regarding race. First, the fact that Dixon plays both parts might be read as a "they all look alike" racial stereotype. That claim, however, could be countered by the number of times the series uses the same devices of disguise and misrecognition with other members of the cast. Second, the fact that the writers had to set up an African storyline before they could interpolate Kinch into a love narrative highlights how attuned they were to his race. Whether or not it was within the imagination of these writers to couple Kinch with the plethora of attractive white women who appear as sexual objects in the series, it is arguable that such a relationship would have exceeded the tolerance of most white viewers in 1966.

By episode 73, "Is General Hammerschlag Burning?" (November 18, 1967), both the American military efforts abroad and racial relations at home had heated up considerably. Inserting a laugh track into representations of these issues became both difficult and necessary. The setup of the episode itself is compelling when read against this backdrop. At a time when Johnson and the U.S. war effort in Vietnam were under severe international criticism for the indiscriminate destruction of North Vietnamese cities, "Is General Hammerschlag Burning?" starts with Hogan being asked to interfere in the Germans' desire to destroy Paris if they are forced to abandon their occupation. Hogan and Kinch go to Paris, where Kinch's former schoolmate Carol Dukes, now known as Kumasa, is a successful nightclub owner and spiritual advisor to the German general in charge of the defense of Paris. They convince General Hammerschlag that Hogan, who is posing as a deaf-mute, can communicate with the spirit of Otto von Bismarck. The general wants to know what the legendary Prussian leader thinks of his military plans for the city. Their ruse allows Kinch and Hogan to gain access to the plans, copy them, and return them to Hammerschlag unnoticed.

When Kinch is trying to convince the general of Hogan's talents, the scene derives its humor from the role reversal in which Hogan must submit to Kinch's extemporizing. In their unrehearsed ruse, Kinch congratulates Hammerschlag on their new discovery:

> Kinch: General, Kumasa has found that this man, in the proper hypnotic state, talks directly with the shade of Prince Bismarck. (*Subtle laugh track.*)
>
> Hammerschlag: But he is a mute you said!
>
> Kinch: Most fascinating, he is . . . a French mute. But under hypnosis his former self emerges, an American of the past century. (*Full laugh track.*)
>
> Hammerschlag: I do not believe it.
>
> Kinch: Kumasa, you remember the prince seemed most interested in the general's career.
>
> Hammerschlag: You mentioned none of this. (*Laugh track.*)
>
> Kinch: It's all been most recent. Look at him, obviously a man of limited intelligence. Observe the eyes, how close together (*Laugh track.*) . . . and yet in the spirit world the intimate of princes.

The exchange carries the tinge of racial connotation, as physiognomy, especially in the hands of Nazi Germans, was employed in their violent racial theories. The joke is that this is being done by a black man to a white man. "Is General Hammerschlag Burning?" allows Kinch to confront the question of what it means to serve a country that does not treat you as an equal. When Kinch works to enlist his former classmate and heartthrob in the effort to thwart the Germans, she inserts race relations directly into the equation.

> Dukes: What makes you think you can casually walk in here and ask me to jeopardize everything I have built all of my life, even risk my life? For what? What?
> Kinch: You'll have to fill that one in yourself.
> Dukes: Ah, for a country that gave me nothing, and I mean not a thing!
> Kinch: Apparently I can't compete with a Nazi general.
> Dukes: He's a pig. But he gives my club protection. And if I could get him in touch with the ghosts of Bismarck, he'd give me Paris.
> Kinch: Wunderbar!

Kinch with Carol Dukes/Kumasa (Barbara McNair), one of his two exoticized romances. ("Is General Hammerschlag Burning?" November 18, 1967)

Dukes: And what's wrong with that? What is wrong with
    looking after number one?

Kinch: Nothing. It sounds like everything is just great. So
    what are you getting so defensive about?

Dukes: Ah, you would be a fool to trust me, you know
    that?

Even coming from an African American character, these anti-patriotic sentiments in a popular prime-time sitcom episode only make sense in an ideological culture in which the ground has been laid for an open rejection of nationalist sentiment. Moreover, the somewhat lengthy exchange marks perhaps the longest stretch in the series in which the laugh track is not deployed. The dispute does not end there, as Dukes/Kumasa never openly offers to help. When the topic is brought up again as to why it is that Kinch is willing to put his life on the line for a country that offers him so little, he demurs an answer. Instead he implores Dukes to reject support for the Nazis, whom she knows to be bad, for the hope that the Americans might serve her better.

"Is General Hammerschlag Burning?" is *Hogan's Heroes*' most overt commentary on race relations. It is easy to see a shift from "The Prince from the Phone Company" two years earlier, when Kinch's race is used as little more than a prop. The Detroit and Newark riots occurred in 1967. The show had long established Kinch as a Detroit native. But placing this discussion between two African Americans from the Motor City about their place within the American patriotic narrative seems at once conservative and progressive. It is reactionary because, despite Dukes's harsh language about owing nothing to her country, the writers never leave any doubt that she will cooperate. Yet her utterances are treated seriously. Kinch's exchange with Dukes may be the most earnest bit of dialogue ever performed in *Hogan's Heroes*. The episode, which deploys an entirely different set from the usual mix of backgrounds, offers slightly higher production values. Edward Feldman, who was the show's long-running executive producer, directed the episode. He uses more camera setups than is usually the case in the series, including in this scene, which uses two cameras. Moreover, Dukes's willingness to help Kinch hardly resolves the underlying conflict that she expresses. Her cooperation reveals itself to be based on an attraction to Kinch.

In Ivan Dixon's last season on the show, *Hogan's Heroes* again broaches the topic of race relations. In episode 126, "The Softer They Fall" (January 23, 1970), Hogan asks Kinch to enter the boxing ring against one of the camp guards, who is purported to be a heavyweight contender.[14] Setting an African American against a German in a boxing ring inevitably invokes the Joe Louis/Max Schmeling rivalry of the 1930s. In fact, along with Jesse Owens's performance at the 1936 Olympics in Berlin, the sports encounters between African American athletes and their ethnic German counterparts served an important historical purpose in invoking a comparison between German and American racism. "The Softer They Fall" acknowledges both of these events.

The episode begins with Klink seeking help in training his entry, "Battling Bruno," in the intercamp boxing tournament. He turns to Kinch to serve as Bruno's sparring partner. Kinch's cooperation will help the POWs in this episode's espionage efforts, which are clearly of secondary narrative importance. The episode concerns itself much more directly with the racial politics of the boxing match. When Kinch knocks out Bruno during their sparring, Burkhalter points out the racial stakes: "A German has been knocked down by an American prisoner of war, and a black prisoner of war at that!" He then demands that Klink organize a proper bout between the two. When Klink hesitates, Burkhalter reminds Klink of Hitler's reaction when Jesse Owens won in Berlin: "Every time he won a gold medal, Hitler left the stadium rather than watch the presentation." He goes on to insist, "It must be known that a German can beat an American at anything." After the POWs complete their caper, Hogan gives the order for Kinch to finish off Bruno. Although Bruno is knocked out, Hogan quickly throws in the towel, claiming Kinch can't go on. This gesture would seem unmotivated within the confines of the episode's story alone. But it sets up one final opportunity for Burkhalter to make a Nazi claim. "You, Sergeant Kinchloe, put up an excellent fight. But the superiority of the master race wins out every time." Thus, the television audience is invited to laugh at Burkhalter's racial buffoonery. Even the normally obsequious Klink finds it ridiculous.

In the twentieth century, sports in general and boxing in particular served as important vehicles for racial integration in the United States. Not only did Joe Louis become arguably the first African American to attain star athlete status in the United States, his efforts, especially in defeating Max Schmeling within the first few minutes of their rematch, dampened Nazi racial propaganda for the moment and made Louis a national hero. Moreover, he paved the way for racial integration that would transform American sports a decade later, in 1947, when Jackie Robinson would break the racial barrier in Major League Baseball. By 1970, when "The Softer They Fall" aired, boxing was again politically charged through the athleticism, flamboyance, and activism of Muhammad Ali, who in 1966 famously opposed the draft stating that "I ain't got no quarrel with the Viet Cong. . . . They never called me a nigger." Ali was put on trial for draft dodging, a process that would drag on for over four years, ending in the Supreme Court in the summer of 1971 as *Hogan's Heroes* was ending its network run. Thus, the plotline alone inserts the episode into some of the most contentious political discussions of the day. It again reveals how adept *Hogan's Heroes*' writers were in using the most sensitive of contemporary cultural currents as fodder for their story lines.

Sketch Comedy and Cartoon Violence

When the film studios began to unload their pre-1948 films to television distributors in 1956, this influx of potential programming material provided an immediate boost both to local network affiliates in need of programming and to the early syndication trade. Associate Artists Productions (AAP) received the distribution rights to Warner Brothers' animated shorts series *Looney Tunes* in that year.[15] Within a few years the cartoons would establish themselves as constant features of syndicated programming. In 1959, the trade journal *Broadcasting* reported United Artists Association general manager Robert Rich's claim that "not one station had failed to renew their initial contract, as 'the cartoons seem to be ageless.'"[16] *Looney Tunes*, along with *The Little Rascals* and *Popeye*, provided local stations with affordable, instant programming for kids.

The *Looney Tunes* provide the most usable model for mapping *Hogan's Heroes* narrative strategy. They also offer the most plausible explanation for why a story about Allied soldiers in a German POW camp would become a big hit with children. Many of the cartoons' characters are set up in the dichotomy of hunter/hunted or predator/prey, whether it is Wile E. Coyote and Roadrunner, Elmer Fudd and Bugs Bunny, or Sylvester and Tweety Bird. In almost every scenario the humor is derived from the extensive violence to which the perpetrator succumbs while hunting his intended victim. The viewer never fears for Tweety Bird's life. The viewer does not perceive the hunter as a real threat. The violence, pranks, and mishaps are all at the predator's expense.

The other lesson to be derived from the misfortunes of Wile E. Coyote and company is the degree of pleasure the viewer derives from the violence done to them. This is initially possible because the viewer presumes that the violence is without consequences. No matter how many anvils fall on Wile E. Coyote's head, he gets back up moments later to continue his hunt.

Klink as a victim of cartoon violence. ("Look at the Pretty Snowflakes," March 21, 1971)

Sylvester may get bonked on the head with a frying pan, but there is no indication that he is suffering anything but frustration. Moreover, within seconds he will continue his pursuit of the speech-impaired little bird with little more injury than momentarily ruffled fur.

Like the *Looney Tunes'* depiction of violence, *Hogan's Heroes* represents aggressions against a not-really-threatening predator. The humor derives from the inversion of the relationship in which the would-be predator becomes the prey. The prisoners effectively rule the camp and easily thwart and occasionally victimize their captors. The ease, predictability, and severity with which the camp prisoners turn the tables on their captors simply enhance the comic inadequacy of the predators and the playful cleverness of the prey. Moreover, the violence itself is much less threatening because it occurs offscreen. If a pompous general must die because he threatens Hogan's sabotage ring, an anvil doesn't fall from the sky. Instead, we hear that his train has exploded from a conversation between Klink and Hogan the next morning. Instead of Roadrunner facing the camera, we get a smugly contemplative look from Hogan while Klink stares at him in confused frustration.

However, an interesting effect of this narrative model in the case of *Hogan's Heroes* is that the bumbling Germans come off as both harmless and sympathetic.[17] Just as the viewer is meant to feel a condescending sympathy and amusement rather than any indignation or anger toward hapless Wile E. Coyote or the ridiculous Elmer Fudd, it is impossible to view the German captors in *Hogan's Heroes* with any form of moral disapproval. It is not that either the coyote or the Germans are presented as well-intentioned or misunderstood nor are they depicted as evil. Rather, whether such was the intention of the show's creators or not, the Germans come off as weak-minded creatures ineptly trying to serve their own self-interest. Their bad intentions simply fall beneath our moral judgment. Anger toward such ineffectual predators would be odd. Indeed, the repetitive nature of the episodes not only reveals the futility of the Germans' various war efforts in the face of Hogan's cunning schemes, the viewer's confidence in Hogan's eventual success actually turns the tables, making the prisoners look like the real sadists. Fan reaction both during the first run and in syndication indicated that the two main German characters, Klink and Schultz, were the viewers' favorites. The predictability of their downfall provides the primary source of humor in the series, not unlike the various tortures endured by Laurel and Hardy or the Three Stooges. It conjures the sort of repetitive humor that is most appealing to children, a characteristic that would both contribute to the eventual demise of the show in its first run and bolster its continued success in syndication.

In reference to humor in the movie theater, Horkheimer and Adorno argued that "the laughter of the cinema is . . . anything but good and revolutionary, instead, *it is full of the worst bourgeois sadism.* . . . With the audience in pursuit, the protagonist becomes the worthless object of general violence. . . . Donald Duck in the cartoons and the unfortunate in real life get their thrashing so the audience can learn to take their own punishment."[18] Even if I leave aside for a moment the argument that screen violence is meant to condition an audience to accept its own violation, the notion that screen humor derives from "bourgeois sadism" might well be operative here. To be sure, when watching Wile E. Coyote attempt to trap Roadrunner, the audience is not only rooting for the bird but is anticipating the hilarity with which the coyote will be crushed, blown up, or otherwise obliterated, only to revive in the next frame. Likewise, when the viewer is enjoying *Hogan's Heroes*, she is doing so for the promise that the prisoners not only will succeed in their mission but also that they will reduce the Germans to worthless objects of violence as they do so. The bourgeois sadism, in this case, may not necessarily result in the viewer learning to accept her own punishment. But perhaps just as troubling, it may result in a sense of superiority in which she believes that others deserve the brutality that is meted out to them. Both *Hogan's Heroes* and *Looney Tunes* make this especially easy by making the object of that violence a Nazi German, coyote, or other predator not apparently worthy of regard.

This, of course, does not reveal some latent American sympathy for the Germans of World War II. Rather, it suggests *Hogan's Heroes*' success, much like that of the various *Looney Tunes* episodes, lies in establishing scenarios in which the events bear little or no relationship to either the physical world or to the history that they reference. It is a sort of wish fulfillment, one particularly relevant during a time of a controversial war, that the enemy is easily identifiable as the predator, and so as a legitimate target of violence, and that combat zones are little more than scenes of inconsequential pranks. As a live-action cartoon, *Hogan's Heroes* found a formula to create humor at the expense of a demographic—namely, wartime Germans—that had even less of an advocacy group than stray cats, coyotes, or speech-impaired hunters. Yet, despite the best intentions of the show's producers, in the guise of a fat and witless sergeant and a blustering colonel, the Germans paradoxically acquire a much friendlier face in American popular culture.

In the next chapter, I will consider what the use of Nazis as victims of situation comedy antics might mean in terms of the series' intervention, if any, into the history and memory of World War II. But, for purposes of determining how *Hogan's Heroes* was narrated, one need only see the Germans as filling the slot of the hunter turned hunted. Moreover, for the sake of continuance, if not continuity, the predator as victim must brush it off and return in the next episode to set himself up again for another humiliation. As such, one can safely say that *Hogan's Heroes'* exaggerated commitment to the generic restrictions of the sitcom, restrictions that encourage repetition and discourage any development across episodes, is key to the construction of its brand of humor.

Removing the History
from World War II

Many stories about the creation of *Hogan's Heroes* have circulated through fan books, websites, and newspapers,[1] yet one version appears authoritative. The creators of *Hogan's Heroes*, Albert Ruddy and Bernard Fein, decided to develop their own version of a military comedy to compete with a planned NBC project. This, as I have already demonstrated, was commonplace programming in the sitcom lineups of the day. The *Campo 44* project, from which the idea for *Hogan's Heroes* was apparently lifted, also seems to have determined that World War II was to be the setting. In attempting to work with prison camp humor and World War II, the creators were, of course, confronted with the severe problem that it was hard to imagine an audience that would find this particular situation humorous. The war was associated not only with a triumphant Allied victory but also a brutal history of atrocities that resulted in millions of deaths. This chapter will show how *Hogan's Heroes* uses various strategies to exploit its historical setting while avoiding the fraught task of actually telling history. The chapter will place the series within the context of the history of the representation of World War II and the Holocaust in both television and film. I will argue that despite its apparent success at circumventing historical narrative, the strategies *Hogan's Heroes* employs result at best in ignorance of, and at worst active interference in, a better understanding of history.

Critics were quick to suggest that a POW camp was an inappropriate setting for a military comedy. The initial review of *Hogan's Heroes* by Jack Gould in the *New York Times* initiates a list of complaints that arose in the subsequent critical reaction to the series: "Every situation comedy requires a generous suspension of belief by a viewer but 'Hogan's Heroes' demands too much."[2] The most cutting of this line of criticism came from the satirical *Mad* magazine. The cartoonish nature of the characters and the premise moved *Mad* in January 1967 to publish the cartoon *Hochman's Heroes* in which concentration camp inmates in Buchenwald are depicted making jokes about their tragic existence. This is where most critics of *Hogan's Heroes* begin and end their discussion of the series. The series was initially panned for both its premise and the cardboard cutout quality of the characters, which would allow for anything to be turned into humor. Jack Gould expressed the fear that "next year we should be ready for Tojo in a family situation comedy."[3] The inherent problem with the show, according to these responses, is an apparent lack of propriety regarding the epistemological value of history. In *Hogan's Heroes*, so the story goes, the goal is never to further historical knowledge about World War II. It does not explore the facts. It does not explore the values at stake and so, arguably, gets those values wrong. It would be hard to argue that such misgivings about the series were misplaced. The series put itself in the position of using history without telling it; but in this respect, *Hogan's Heroes* was far from unique.

The use of World War II as a setting for television shows was not new. In the 1960s era, television programmers found the war to be a rich field for developing serial storylines. *Combat!*, an action drama series about an infantry squad in the European war zone, ran on ABC from 1962 to 1967, cracking the top ten in Nielsen ratings in the 1964–65 season. ABC paired the dramatic series with *McHale's Navy*, a situation comedy about a PT boat in the Pacific. Two years later *Combat!* ran alongside *Twelve O'Clock High*, which was a serialization of Twentieth Century Fox's 1949 hit film and dramatized the exploits of a bomber squadron flying in Europe. All of these series seem intended to capitalize on a renewed interest in the history of World War II that occupied parts of American culture in the first half of the decade. The most obvious manifestation of this interest was Twentieth Century Fox's successful (and much more historically ambitious) film *The Longest Day* (Ken Annakin, 1962). In the second half of this chapter, I will retrace the various cinematic legacies from which *Hogan's Heroes* draws and to which it contributes.

Insofar as World War II serves as less a historical and more a fantastical backdrop for *Hogan's Heroes*, the Holocaust is a bit like an apparition that haunts the series without ever allowing itself to be seen. The series quite studiously avoids discussion of the Nazis' worst crimes to sustain the ground for its cartoonish humor. It does, however, make constant reference to the German war machine and the range of its destructive capability, and this is precisely what the POWs are out to destroy. Arguably, if it avoids discussion of German crimes against humanity, the series foregrounds German military might and the state security apparatus. But *Hogan's Heroes* uses these historical institutions—whether they are the Luftwaffe, the SS, or the Gestapo—as little more than prefabricated foils. The show studiously avoids revealing the actual historical atrocities these organizations committed. Although a great portion of the generation that participated in World War II was still alive at the time *Hogan's Heroes* was shown, a wider popular understanding of the brutal history of the Third Reich was only beginning to take hold.

In 1965 when *Hogan's Heroes* was conceived, historical discourse about the Holocaust was in its nascency. Raul Hilberg's

The Destruction of the European Jews was published in 1961. While that book is widely understood as marking the beginning of true historical analysis of the Holocaust, it certainly did not make an immediate impact. Also in 1961, Adolf Eichmann was tried in Jerusalem for his role in the planning and execution of the Holocaust. As Jeffrey Shandler puts it, "The Eichmann trial . . . was the first major public effort to conceptualize the Holocaust as a discrete chapter of history, distinguished from larger narratives of World War II or the Third Reich, and defined as a phenomenon centered around Nazi efforts to exterminate Jews."[4] The trial was televised in America and facilitated a wide variety of television documentaries on all three networks regarding Nazi history and the Holocaust.

In this way, by 1962, the Holocaust had found its way, however temporarily, onto American television and had begun to make inroads into the American historical consciousness. However, serious treatment of the phenomenon had yet to emerge in the American cinema. George Stevens's *The Diary of Anne Frank* premiered to moderate success in 1959 but offered a family melodrama with the offscreen threat of Nazi persecution rather than a concentration camp story. Sidney Lumet's *The Pawnbroker* (1964) marks one of the earliest American treatments of the memory of the camps. But despite a strong critical response, the film fared poorly at the box office. The wide range of filmic narratives that would test the range of stories that could or should be told about the Holocaust would emerge after *Hogan's Heroes'* run had ended. A much longer period of time had to pass before credible (and still controversial) attempts to make comedies set in the Holocaust appeared in Western cinema, such as Roberto Benigni's *Life Is Beautiful* (1997) and Peter Kassovitz's 1999 remake of the 1975 East German film *Jakob the Liar* (Frank Beyer). The undeveloped state of historical discourse in the mid-1960s suggests why *Hogan's Heroes'* producers would have wanted to steer clear of the topic.

To appreciate *Hogan's Heroes'* relationship to historical discourse, one must first understand the limits of both sitcoms and traditional television programming. With numerous cable television channels now dedicated to historical narrative of one type or another, it is hard to imagine that television was not always a major source of Americans' basic historical knowledge. But the genre of historical melodrama, at least of the variety that has any pretenses toward historical accuracy, and which is now a staple on the History Channel, was not really established for television until ABC's 1977 eight-part miniseries, *Roots*. A year later NBC hired the series' director, Marvin Chomsky, to take up another historical miniseries, *Holocaust*. The series succeeded tremendously in the ratings yet set off a firestorm of controversy, both at home and abroad, about the appropriateness of dramatizing this subject matter for commercial television.

The most famous of the responses to *Holocaust* was from survivor and eventual Nobel laureate Elie Wiesel, who concluded his scathing critique of the miniseries by noting, "The Holocaust must be remembered. But not as a show."[5] Perhaps even more damning was the second of two reviews of the series by *New York Times* television critic John J. O'Connor. O'Connor went beyond his aesthetic panning from the first review and discussed the effect of depicting the horrors of the Holocaust between commercial breaks.

> The television system . . . is forced to do business as usual, and in the case of "Holocaust," that means a slew of commercials punctuating a story of sadistic torture and prolonged suffering. . . . A story that includes victims being told that the gas chambers are only disinfecting areas is interrupted for a message about Lysol and its usefulness in "killing germs." After several scenes of perverted Nazi officers looking at photographs of mass murders, we are given a sales pitch for Polaroid.[6]

With this critique, O'Connor questions how a medium that depends on shilling consumer products might ever be able to approach legitimately the serious philosophical and aesthetic issues that haunt the histories of both slavery and the Shoah.[7] However, such criticism notwithstanding, the success of *Roots* and *Holocaust* further cemented the cultural legitimacy of 1970s-era television.

The miniseries format allowed television to do something that it had been hard pressed to accomplish in other formats— namely, produce relatively traditional historical fiction that could tell a story with a fixed end point. No matter how seriously a conventional television series may try, its basic format will hinder it from consistently producing a storyline that would reasonably qualify as historical fiction. The length of a series depends on its ability to earn ratings. An unsuccessful series would not be allowed to continue its narrative and a successful series had to be milked at least long enough to be viable for syndication. Even if one were to view *M*A*S*H* as the paradigm for historical television in the conventional serial format, the series offers us little insight into the actual history of the Korean War. At best, individual episodes make reference to or use of particular moments in history as plot devices. The narrative employs a historical setting; it does not attempt to expand the viewer's understanding of a particular historical event, period, or situation. The serial format, at least as it is used in American television, forces writers to eschew a teleological narrative in which the story's end is visable.[8] In general, the historical comedy experiences a severe drop-off in the 1970s.[9] *M*A*S*H* represents the last successful American uniform situation comedy.

Legitimizing Laughter

Knowing that comedic portrayals of Nazis and POWs would raise eyebrows, the series' producers systematically and prominently publicized the cast members' own, blameless connections to that history. Not only were four regular cast members (Werner Klemperer, John Banner, Leon Askin, and Howard Caine) veterans of the war in the American armed forces, but four members were also, to varying degrees, victims of the Nazi persecution of Jews. In the buildup to the show's premiere, public relations maneuvers seem designed to set up the cast members as legitimizers who would grant the television audience the permission to laugh.[10] And, indeed, these cast members had stories that were well suited to that purpose.

Werner Klemperer (Colonel Klink) was the son of the famous German conductor Otto Klemperer. When the National Socialists came to power in 1933, the family immigrated first to Vienna and then to the United States. The Klemperers were among the first members of the German Jewish exile community in Southern California that would eventually include noted filmmakers, composers, actors, and academicians such as Fritz Lang, Arnold Schoenberg, Fritz Kortner, Theodor Adorno, and Max Horkheimer. Novelist Thomas Mann and playwright Bertolt Brecht would also form influential components of this German exile community. Before taking up an acting career, Werner Klemperer became an accomplished violinist, a skill purposely suppressed in the numerous episodes where Klink exhibits more dilettantism than mastery of the instrument.

Because of his family's rapid exit from Nazi Germany, Werner Klemperer may have been the least directly affected of all of *Hogan's Heroes*' European-born cast members. John Banner (Sergeant Schultz), who was roughly ten years older than Klemperer, was born to a Viennese Jewish family. He began his career at the Volkstheater in Vienna and was on tour in Zurich with that company in 1938 when the Germans rolled into Austria.[11] The Nazi annexation of his homeland thus also forced Banner to immigrate first to New York and then to Southern California where, like many thickly accented German or Austrian Jewish exiled actors, he would be consigned to playing Nazis.

Banner's biography is quite similar to that of his fellow rotund Austrian castmate, Leon Askin. Having studied in the famous drama school directed by Max Reinhardt, Askin enjoyed a more prominent stage career than Banner.[12] Askin was working in Düsseldorf when the Nazis came to power and, like many Jews in public positions, was fired immediately. Shortly thereafter, he was arrested and beaten by the Gestapo before being released, thanks to his Austrian citizenship, and allowed to leave Germany for France.[13] In 1935, Askin, then still Leo Aschkenasy, returned to Vienna, only to then flee when the Nazis annexed Austria in March 1938. In 1939, after the war began, he was detained in a French internment camp because, ironically, he was officially a citizen of the Third Reich. Friends finally arranged for him to be released from the camp in 1940 and to emigrate to the United States.[14] Thus, like Banner and Klemperer, Askin left Europe under the cloud of Nazi persecution.

No one in the *Hogan's Heroes* cast had as much unwelcome contact with the Nazi apparatus as did Robert Clary (Corporal LeBeau). Born Robert Widermann to an Orthodox Jewish family of Polish immigrants in Paris on March 1, 1926, his was the most improbable journey to the set of *Hogan's Heroes*.[15] Clary spent almost three years in a variety of German concentration camps before finally being liberated from Buchenwald in April 1945. During his stay in Buchenwald, Clary had begun to sing in a small combo that entertained the other inmates. After the war, Clary started a career as a nightclub singer, first doing an Al Jolson–like blackface show. In 1948, Clary made a couple of recordings that became hits in America. This led to his move to the United States the next year. Upon his arrival Clary bounced around, playing several nightclub gigs and appearing in small films. His breakthrough came with a Broadway musical revue called *New Faces of 1952* (later just called *New Faces*) that also served to launch the careers of Paul Lynde and Eartha Kitt. In addition, Clary benefited from the friendship of vaudevillian Eddie Cantor, who would eventually become his father-in-law. By his own admission, he received the role on *Hogan's Heroes* because he was a diminutive Frenchman. While it was obvious that they needed a French member of the ensemble, his short stature added to his comic appeal.

The biographies of these four actors matter because these men were involved not only in a historical comedy but one that became controversial because of its subject matter. The European cast members expressed both reservations about their work and defenses of it. I have already noted Kinsky's objections, which led to his quick exit from the cast. In an interview, John Banner dismissed the criticism of the series by drawing a parallel to *Arsenic and Old Lace*, the dark comedy in which a couple of little old ladies turn into serial murderers. Banner goes on to suggest a reading of the series that I will take up again in chapter 3: "We will always be able to laugh at someone

Robert Clary as LeBeau offers a mock salute to Carter's Hitler imitation, yet crosses his fingers ("Will the Real Adolf Please Stand Up?" December 2, 1966)

flaunting authority."[16] Banner also asserts in the same interview that he "believes it is wonderful to be able to laugh about militarism." While Kinsky's concern was that the series was too flippant given the seriousness of the history to which it tentatively referred, Banner suggests that *Hogan's Heroes* is really not referring to history at all.

The life stories of the actors were also exploited to verify that the *Hogan's Heroes* production was perfectly aware of the serious history of World War II and German atrocities. Both Banner and Klemperer gave interviews explicitly defending the story line that they were simultaneously creating. Either the producers were selective in their deployment of these stories or they were unaware of the most difficult history in the bunch, namely Clary's. This could either have been because Clary's initial role in the series was not large enough to warrant using him for publicity appearances or because Clary's actual history as a concentration camp inmate was much more serious and difficult to reconcile with the demands of a sitcom than Klemperer's and Banner's escape stories. The producers needed these stories in order to say, "Listen, we aren't ignorant of the history." More importantly, they were saying, "If these people say it is okay to laugh, then it is okay to laugh. If they think this is okay, then who are you to complain?" This is, in some ways, analogous to racial humor in the United States in which comedians from minority groups invoke epithets or describe situations in a manner that would be inappropriate for those not belonging to that particular demographic. In the case of *Hogan's Heroes*, the creators had a formula for comedy with which they were able to succeed in spite of rather than because of the history in which it was set.

Hogan's Heroes and Historical Discourse

Despite the connection that many in the production had to its historical setting, *Hogan's Heroes* is more adept at avoiding actual reference to World War II than it is at engaging it. But its occlusion of history is not complete. The series' creators and writers had to develop a sophisticated strategy for invoking a particular historical moment without actually engaging in that moment's history. For much of the humor to work, the writers relied on a certain common understanding of Germans during World War II. Germans (or at least a certain class of them) needed to be irredeemably evil to justify the cartoon violence that would be wrought upon them week after week. But elucidating what the Nazis did to deserve the "evil" label would have undermined the series' ability to perform the sort of broad-stroke comedy for which it clearly aims. Understanding how *Hogan's Heroes* accomplishes this complicated dance is a step toward comprehending the consequences of the series' strained relationship to the past.

The most obvious ways in which *Hogan's Heroes* deploys the past is both as a source of props and a generator of stock characters. The series takes some of the most clichéd character portraits (heartless Germans, weak French, bumbling or dodgy Brits, and deceptive Russians) and turns them into skit material. More rarely, events such as the D-day invasion or the 1944 conspiracy to kill Hitler are used, although they serve as little more than set pieces to decorate stock plots in which the prisoners outwit the Germans in the service of a comic routine. Comedy is not used to better understand history; history is used to create more effective comedy.

Another strategy that *Hogan's Heroes* employs to foreswear any type of realistic depiction of the past is to remove temporal causality from the historical narrative. Because the series does not develop a consistent story arc, the historical events it uses appear as having no causal relationship to one another. Not only does time's arrow occasionally get blunted or sent back in the other direction, the sum of actions that have been portrayed in previous episodes rarely offer a prehistory to what will happen in later ones. The Germans seem to continually fall for the same traps, disguises, or diversions. The weather never changes. (There are always patches of snow on the ground, and current high-definition technology reveals the actors are frequently sweating.) Rather than a teleologically constructed timeline, the series offers a sort of constellation of events among which one is meant to draw arbitrary connections. What emerges from this history without time is a sense of war as a permanent condition.

This treatment of history also plays itself out at the level of individual episodes and the narrative motivation for each week's exploit. In almost every episode, the inmates are confronted with a task of such critical importance that the balance of the war allegedly hangs on its successful completion. A bridge must be blown up, battle plans must be captured, or a munitions factory must be destroyed lest the Germans gain an irreversible strategic advantage. By the end of each episode, the task has been accomplished and the Germans are defeated for the day. But, however crucial the prisoners' mission may have been, however heroic the exploit, it has no lasting impact on history. History remains a collection of contingent events that do not build on one another. And it encourages the audience to think of the war not as a causal chain of events but as a random cluster of violent acts. Having adopted such an attitude about history, the show renders absurd all discourse about war.

The very conceit that historical events have no causal relationship with one another can be read in a different light as well. Historical contingency as an organizing principle in *Hogan's Heroes* works alongside a rescaling of historical engagement. The result is a "little guy" theory of history. Every time an episode claims that the outcome of the war will turn on the prisoners' ability to pull off a particular stunt, the show suggests that history is made not in the halls of power but in the sphere of influence occupied by common people. The outcome of the episodes, and even the global historical events to which they claim to be attached, hinges on the vicissitudes of a particular act or interpersonal tie.

"D-Day at Stalag 13" offers us a glimpse into the little guy theory turned into narrative hypothesis. In this case, the question is, What would D-day have been like if Klink were in charge of the German forces? At the same time, the episode shows how the series might have functioned differently. Hogan travels briefly to London to receive a debriefing on the upcoming invasion plans. Hogan's British commander then gives him a task that fits into the overall strategy. Hogan is meant to contrive a situation to distract the German high command so that when the invasion happens they will not be able to respond. This plan is a riff on a scenario played out in *The Longest Day* in which high command officers are depicted as waiting around for Hitler to wake up before launching a counterattack on the Allied forces. The POWs contrive to cause the general staff to believe that an angry Hitler has fired his chief of staff and hired Klink to replace him. They accomplish this improbable ruse through Newkirk's Hitler imitation and with the help of a spy who had been planted years earlier as the wife of the current chief. The prisoners exploit her intimacy with the general to carry out their scheme. By the time the matter is cleared up, the Allies have landed successfully at Normandy, the wife is sent to England, and Klink is restored to his harmless Stalag 13 post.

This episode offers a counternarrative to *The Longest Day*, a film that depicts the invasion of Normandy from the top down. While the film does offer numerous vignettes of foot soldiers, resistance fighters, and brave citizens, the overall narrative is structured more like a chess game in which general officers are moving the pieces. *Hogan's Heroes*, on the other hand, sets up a game where the little guys of Stalag 13, with the help of an insider, essentially hijack the German generals' pieces. By retelling the heroics of June 6, 1944, from this absurd position, the episode presents the same ahistorical stance as the rest of the series.

Before taking the notion of *Hogan's Heroes* as a history of the everyman's contribution to the outcome of World War II too far, one would do well to note that the group of prisoners appears to be metonymic for the Allied forces as a whole (minus the Russian, Minsk, whose symbolic position as one of the core group of prisoners was never refilled.) In other words, the prisoners might not necessarily be seen as individuals but stand-ins for larger groups. The series establishes its ensemble in a manner similar to the trope in the combat film genre in which the company of GIs embodies the American myth of the melting pot. Jeanine Basinger describes this typical company as "the military unit of enlisted men and officers—separated by rank, education, background, and lifestyles."[17] In this case, the national tensions between particular groups often play themselves out in the personal tensions among characters. This metonymy might have been even more effective (and perhaps even more blatantly political) had Leonid Kinsky remained in the cast. Nevertheless, the series utilizes Newkirk, LeBeau, and the Americans in that same light, animating the Brit and the Frenchman in frequent cultural disputes that highlight both the common stereotypes and competing interests of the two Allies. Although the American Sergeant Carter often becomes embroiled in the same bickering dynamic, the insults thrown at him are generally confined to his intelligence or supposed lack thereof and not to his status as an American. Hogan, as senior officer and American, is the Eisenhower of the group, the natural leader. This remains true even in the Crittendon episodes, where the clumsy British colonel outranks him. Part of the humor is derived from the notion that a Brit might lead Americans during war. Even the metonymic setup of the primary Allied powers in the camp does not undermine the ahistoricity. Rather, it allows the series to function much more like a family sitcom with a preestablished set of sibling tensions. *Hogan's Heroes* presents a small family led by the paternal American and, as such, offers a precursor to the sitcoms beginning in the 1970s in which the family metaphor is extended to include the workplace, of which *Mary Tyler Moore*, *Alice* (CBS, 1975–85), or *WKRP in Cincinnati* (CBS, 1978–82) are typical.

If *Hogan's Heroes* does not engage in history telling regarding World War II, would it have been conceivable without the war? In other words, what position does the war play in the series? If *Hogan's Heroes* offers anything critical to historical discourse, it may well be the controversial suggestion that World War II was not a unique phenomenon but itself nothing more than an episode. The show offers a cyclical take on history in which the current crisis is little more than a return of the last one. It is a classic illustration of the words with which Karl Marx opens "The Eighteenth Brumaire of Louis Bonaparte": "Hegel says somewhere that great historic facts and personages recur twice. He forgot to add: 'Once as tragedy, and again as farce.'"[18] For *Hogan's Heroes*, history is, among other things, a long succession of wars in which the last war keeps returning as a farce in the next one. They might have dressed up the characters in World War II garb in this series, but they could have just as easily clothed them in Roman tunics or the blues and grays of the American Civil War.

The credit sequence of all episodes after the pilot features a shot of the Prussian military helmet, the *Pickelhaube*, that Klink keeps on his desk, being used as a hat rack for Hogan's own much more modern officer's cap. This reference to the military dress uniform that went out of fashion at the end of World War I offers us at least two possible interpretations. It seems unlikely that the makers of *Hogan's Heroes* were so historically ignorant to believe that this was a part of Nazi-era garb. A more plausible interpretation is that the show plugs into the long and illustrious career that the *Pickelhaube* enjoyed in the anti-German propaganda of World War I in England and the United States. It became shorthand for Prussian militarism and warmongering, enough that the helmet retained its currency fifty years later. Set up as an obvious object of Klink's pride and longing for the glory days that never were, Hogan frequently uses the helmet as a prop with which to light a match, clean out a pipe, or hide a listening device. The viewer is thereby led to perceive the helmet as a sign of Klink's attachment to an unmodern world and an outmoded military order pitted against Hogan's more relaxed and resourceful espionage acumen.

World War I returns as a topic in a number of episodes. In "The Rise and Fall of Sergeant Schultz" (October 21, 1966), we are told that in the earlier war the bumbling sergeant heroically saved his whole company, including a young officer who has now become a general. In "Will the Blue Baron Strike Again" (December 14, 1968), Klink's inglorious history as a failed fighter pilot in World War I is revealed. Although he is a Luftwaffe officer, it is obvious that all of Klink's battle experience came from a war waged thirty years earlier. In both cases, German military history is one long march apparently uninter-

Hogan cracks a walnut with Klink's *Pickelhaube*. ("Hold That Tiger," September 24, 1965)

rupted by the sixteen years from 1919 to 1935 when the nation was disarmed.

The attitude about war as a continuum and not a discrete event had crept into combat films in the last years of World War II. *Hogan's Heroes* takes this attitude for granted. Characters often refer to how something went in the last war or what they will do differently in the next one. In episode 59, "The Tower" (March 17, 1967), Burkhalter tells Klink that perhaps the latter will finally be a general in the next war. In the same episode, LeBeau remarks, "I hope the next war will be friendlier than this one." Every such remark is underlined with a laugh track. As the frequency of these particular comments increased over time, one is led to wonder at what the audience was meant to be laughing. As I will discuss in more depth in chapter 3, *Hogan's Heroes* is a television series set in World War II about a German military that imagines itself fighting World War I and a band of saboteurs fighting an underground insurrection that looks a lot like the war that was being waged when the series was made and aired.

Hogan's Heroes' employment of a historical understanding that avoided representations of trauma is typical of its time in television history. The same patterns of avoidance can be seen in other military comedies of the era. *F Troop* did not attempt to represent the wholesale slaughter of native peoples in the West after the Civil War, *McHale's Navy* did not set out to portray the devastating war in the Pacific, and *Gomer Pyle, U.S.M.C.* did not remind viewers that mid-1960s Marine recruits were likely headed for a deadly conflict in Southeast Asia. Such was simply not the forum of the situation comedy, especially in the heavily physical slapstick comedy style of the mid-1960s. In *Hogan's Heroes* the most brutal threats are those the Germans aim at one another—namely, a reassignment to the Russian front. Thus, the real brutality is to be found offscreen in Russia, not Germany.

How does treating the facts of the war lightly affect the audience's ability to understand and make use of that past? Television studies often inspire scholars to reveal how they themselves make or have made use of this rather personal medium. In my case, I fit precisely the demographic of the children who grew up watching *Hogan's Heroes*, both toward the end of its network run and for years after in syndication. My friends and I responded most positively to the stylized performances of John Banner, Werner Klemperer, and Leon Askin whose uniformed German characters were the show's comic centerpieces. We would affect heavy accents and claim to "know nasing" or "have vays ov making you talg" à la Schultz or Burkhalter. We knew little then about the Holocaust or the Nazi regime and certainly did not associate these comedic characters with that ugly history. That is perhaps the point and the problem.

Hogan's Heroes neither mentions the word "Jew," nor portrays anyone as Jewish, nor mentions the atrocities that occurred in "camps" with other names. As noted, it is not surprising that the writers would eschew reference to the Holocaust in their broad sitcom narrative. The stock character of the combat films, the Jewish kid from Brooklyn (Harry Shapiro in *Stalag 17*), becomes the diminutive cook from Paris instead. The avoidance of any mention of Jews is perhaps most interesting when it comes to the episodes whose plots center on helping someone escape from Germany. In the frequently repeated plotlines mentioned earlier, such as blowing up German infrastructure or stealing the latest technology from the Nazis, aiding escapes was one of the main occupations of the POWs. Historically, the most populous group of people who were in fact trying desperately to escape from Germany during the war were those in danger of being sent to the concentration camps, and most of these people were Jews. It is easy to understand why the writers avoided telling this variant of an escape story, but they had to populate their plots with someone. So, in addition to a series of downed Allied pilots, the escape episodes collectively represent a large number of German dissidents and defectors who need Hogan's help to get to England, where they will further contribute to the Allied cause. Indeed, the German populace ends up looking like an ally in the war against the Nazis. Most of the civilian Germans in the series—the dog keeper who smuggles prisoners in and out of the camp, various wives or daughters of the military elite, the camp secretary and the waitresses at the local bar—are depicted as part of an apparently vast antiregime underground. Even the German shepherd dogs are in the resistance. Thus, local hostility toward the regime looks much more like wartime France than wartime Germany.

The final problem regarding the avoidance of historical trauma concerns the series' perhaps most sympathetic character, Sergeant Schultz, and the utterances for which he was most famous. From the pilot episode onward, the series implicates Schultz in the prisoners' shenanigans. Each time the dim-witted sergeant witnesses the POWs preparing to pull off a stunt, he bellows his famous "I know nothing. I see nothing." This is, of course, intended to depict Schultz's passive solidarity with the Allied cause. But, it is possible to view this willful ignorance differently.

One of the most common refrains of Germans in the immediate postwar period, when confronted by the horrors wrought upon others in their name, was to claim to have known nothing and to have seen nothing. Because of the degree to which the National Socialists went, especially as the war began to turn for the worse, to implicate wide swaths of the military and general society in the atrocities they were committing, this claim rings about as true as Schultz's. But as *Hogan's Heroes'* most famous punch line from its most loveable character, the heavily German-accented expression of willful ignorance tends to disarm our judgment when it comes out of the mouths of real members of the regime.

The question is then not just what it means to treat the brutal history of World War II as sitcom fodder but also what

Schultz closes his eyes to the heroes' antics. ("The Battle of Stalag 13," October 14, 1966)

it means to trivialize wartime Germans in the process. Herein arguably lies the most influential and the most troubling aspect of *Hogan's Heroes*. Until *Holocaust* in 1978 or the Herman Wouk franchises *Winds of War* and *War and Remembrance* in the 1980s, *Hogan's Heroes* was the most extensive treatment of

Germans during World War II to appear on American television.[19] When we recognize that legacy, we better understand what was at stake in the miniseries *Holocaust*. As opposed to the long and complicated combination of films produced about the war for the big screen, American television had, throughout the 1960s, yet to come up with a sustained historical discourse about World War II, let alone the Holocaust. And until it did, *Hogan's Heroes* offered a weekly image of wartime Germans that was compatible with the postwar relationship that the United States was actively cultivating with West Germany.

Hogan's Heroes went on the air ten years after the Federal Republic of Germany was admitted into the North Atlantic Treaty Organization. The construction of the Berlin Wall in 1961 created even more solidarity between the United States and its vanquished former enemy; it quite literally cemented West Germany as a reliable ally in the Cold War. This was also an era in which it is widely accepted that Germans were doing little themselves to investigate their relationship to their Nazi past, either individually or collectively.[20] Thus, despite the fact that the show hardly paints Germans in a flattering light, the airing of a popular television series that elided the violence that Germans committed against themselves and most of the rest of Europe did no harm to German-American relations. By the time the series ended, however, even Germany was insisting on a more direct confrontation with its Nazi past.

Hogan's Heroes' Cinematic Cousins

Hogan's Heroes was not created in a cultural vacuum. Not only did it emerge in the context of the many uniform and spy comedies that proliferated in the mid-1960s network television schedule, it also drew from a twenty-five-year history of cinematic depictions of World War II. Moreover, the popularity of the show influenced subsequent filmic discourse about the war and its narrative representation. There were, of course, dozens of war films made in the period. The remainder of this chapter will trace the films that are particularly relevant to *Hogan's Heroes* and demonstrate how the series continues to play a part in cinematic discourse.

Even before America entered the war, Hollywood studios had begun a counteroffensive against Hitler's Germany. Warner Brothers used World War I as a backdrop to reintroduce the notion of the brave citizen-soldier in *Sergeant York* (Howard Hawks, 1940) over a year before the Pearl Harbor attacks. Once World War II began, the close cooperation between the Office of War Information and the film industry resulted in a range of films that supported both the military efforts abroad and the necessary sacrifices at home. Films such as *Bataan* (Tay Garnett, 1943) and *Wake Island* (John Farrow, 1942) were used to explain the events that had been presented months before in newsreels. This first wave of films about the war dramatized the fact that the war would be long and hard and would entail losses as well as victories.

As the war drew to a close, films such as *The Story of G.I. Joe* (William A. Wellman, 1945) and *A Walk in the Sun* (Lewis Milestone, 1945) began to look at the toll that the mounting victories had taken on those who achieved them. The most lauded film of this second wave, *The Best Years of Our Lives* (William Wyler, 1946), examines whether or not the victory achieved was worth the personal pain and sacrifice. These films echoed widespread public fatigue with the war and its costs. Wyler's film directly confronted the question of how to reintegrate soldiers into civilian life.

Jeanine Basinger identifies the third wave of World War II films with those combat films made in the decade or so after the war's end, such as William A. Wellman's *Battleground* (1949). These films "bring the war down-to-earth, removing the 'why we fight' propaganda of the war years and treating those who fought it like fallible human beings who are rising to the occasion out of the instincts of survival."[21] Some of these films were made during the Korean War and suggest a reluctance to reengage in the rhetoric of war.

Around this time, two films appeared that would become primary source material for *Hogan's Heroes*. Both *Stalag 17* (Billy Wilder, 1953) and *The Great Escape* (John Sturges, 1963) are set in Luftwaffe POW camps. Both portray escape plans that go terribly awry, the latter with considerably less humor. Bob Crane seems to mimic James Garner's cool demeanor as Lieutenant Hendley in *The Great Escape*. The most obvious poaching, however, comes from *Stalag 17*. The writers of the play on which Wilder's film was based were apparently so convinced of an obvious plagiarism on the part of the creators of *Hogan's Heroes* that they filed an unsuccessful lawsuit.[22] The soldier in charge of the barracks is named Schultz, something that one of the teleplay writers, Richard Powell, claimed to have lifted from Ernst Lubitsch's *To Be or Not to Be* (1942).[23] Both German-born Sig Ruman and John Banner play their Schultz in strikingly similar manners. The acting style of Leon Askin in his role as General Burkhalter draws from Otto Preminger's portrayal of the Stalag 17 camp commandant, Colonel von Scherbach; both actors play their parts in English with heavy German accents, something that even non-German-speaking actors mimic.

The release of *The Longest Day* in 1962 marks a fourth wave in the filmic representations of World War II, which becomes the equilibrium point reached by the wartime generation. *The Longest Day* represents an insistence on a hallowed image of the war by the generation that fought it to their children's generation. The film asserts this attitude by fleshing out the picture of all of the sides of the invasion at Normandy, while creating an image of unquestioned American military and ideological superiority. This film is often read as the war generation's filmic claim on its political legacy at a moment just before that legacy would be called into question.

While the films of the fourth wave were generally historical reenactment combat films, the bent toward lionization is also seen in the 1965 historical fantasy film *Von Ryan's Express* (Mark Robson, 1965), which, as a POW camp film, was also influential on *Hogan's Heroes*. The film opens with Colonel Joseph Ryan (Frank Sinatra) being taken to an Italian POW camp. There he suffers the resentment of his mostly British fellow inmates because he thwarts their many attempts at escape. They dub him "Von Ryan" because they believe that he is collaborating with the enemy. When the Germans invade Italy and take over the camp, they attempt to transfer all of the POWs to a German camp. En route over the Alps, Ryan and his fellow prisoners hijack the train and reroute it toward Switzerland. Colonel Ryan sacrifices himself in the end to ensure that the train filled with his comrades makes it over the border.

While the film retains the heroic status of the World War II veteran, it presages *Hogan's Heroes* engagement in historical fantasy. *Von Ryan's Express* depicts Germans and Italians as bumbling and inept. The prisoners don Wehrmacht uniforms and manage to pass as Germans, though only one in their group speaks German. They resort to zany tactics (burning all their clothes) to thwart their camp commanders. In the end, not only do they hijack the train that is to transport them to a camp in Germany, they manage to reroute it, circumnavigate Milan, and storm the Swiss border. Though the film is much more serious than *Hogan's Heroes*, it displays the same willingness to skirt empirical reality for dramatic and comedic effect.

The Longest Day and the other films of the fourth wave provide a narrative baseline out of which *Hogan's Heroes* will create its fantasy. In this shared worldview, the Americans are morally infallible, the Germans are stupid and misled, and the other Allies are junior partners. Yet during the run of *Hogan's Heroes*, the basic premise of American moral superiority would undergo radical questioning. *Hogan's Heroes* enters relatively early into a cultural conversation being conducted in the cinema that reshapes the lens through which World War II and those who fought it are viewed by the postwar generation.

Joseph Heller's 1961 novel *Catch 22* became one of the most influential novels of that decade. As a careful study of bureaucratic and authoritarian reasoning, it gained influence as younger Americans began to protest American involvement in Vietnam. By the time Mike Nichols's adaptation of the novel hit the silver screen in 1970, both the film and novel were primed to become the definitive voice for the frustration with the dominant fictions of World War II, a frustration fueled by the war in Vietnam. Thus from *Hogan's Heroes'* network premiere in September 1965 to the end of its run in July 1971, it had become part of a discursive shift away from a critical historical reverence to a much more contested view of American history.

Another film that picks up the premise of prisoners reentering battle in World War II is *The Dirty Dozen* (Robert Aldrich, 1967), which appeared two years into *Hogan's Heroes'* run. In this case, however, the inmates are not prisoners of war but condemned convicts who are given a chance at freedom if they volunteer for a suicide mission on D-day. Their mission is to capture a chateau behind enemy lines used by German officers for R&R and kill everyone inside, civilian or military. The typical fighting family developed in the combat film sought to include the ethnic and geographical diversity of America. Here it is transformed into a unit of hardened criminals willing to kill indiscriminately.

A British spin on the topic of criminals at war, *Play Dirty* (André De Toth), premiered in 1968. This time, not only are the criminals more hardened and cynical, but the war effort itself has been privatized and is exposed as a venture for corporate gain. In this much more violent film, the saboteurs are malicious and backstabbing, not interested in the ideals of the war effort. A combat film mired in the politics of the Vietnam era, *Play Dirty* reflects the disillusionment resulting from the conflict in Southeast Asia.

The film that drew most heavily from the antics of *Hogan's Heroes* is Brian Hutton's *Kelly's Heroes* (1970). Its premise, to sneak in behind enemy lines and capture (and keep) $16 million worth of gold bullion, picks up on a *Hogan's Heroes* episode ("The Gold Rush," January 14, 1966) and uses a similar mix of irreverence and comedy to animate the caper. Here, too, instead of a monumental generational sacrifice, World War II is reduced to a criminal heist.

Inglorious Bastards (*Quel maledetto treno blindato*; Enzo Castellari, 1978) most obviously took its cue from *The Dirty Dozen* and *Hogan's Heroes*. In this film from which Quentin Tarantino would derive the title of his 2009 film, criminals are again sent on a war mission. The mission, to steal a bit of German war technology for the underground, and the comedic portrayals look much like the television series. Seven years after the end of *Hogan's Heroes'* network run the irreverence toward the World War II referent that the series established continued to live on in this "spaghetti combat film."

Hogan's Heroes maintains a paradoxical relationship to all of these narrative strands. Although it remains relatively steadfast in its heroic depiction of World War II, that depiction includes from the start antiauthoritarian tendencies similar to *The Dirty Dozen*, elements of comic unorthodoxy that clearly influence *Kelly's Heroes*, and it shares with *Catch 22* a depiction of war as an infinite loop in which no progress is really made and no end is in sight.

Hogan's Heroes was not only part of a culture of World War II caper films, it spawned at least one production of its own. In 1968, the principals of *Hogan's Heroes*—Crane, Banner, Klemperer, and Askin—took part in a film project in which they essentially removed their characters from the historical World War II scenario to the contemporary Cold War one. In *The Wicked Dreams of Paula Schultz* (George Marshall), Crane plays a con artist, Bill Mason, who is on the lamb from creditors when he encounters a beautiful and mostly naked East German sports star, Paula Schultz (Elke Sommer). He at first uses her to scam East German officials, played by Klemperer, Askin, and Banner, but ultimately falls in love with her. This causes him to scam the officials again, so that they both might escape East Berlin for West. Most of the parts of the *Hogan's Heroes* formula remain intact, including Klemperer, who mimics his decrying of "Schultz," this time referring to the scantily clad athlete. The three German officials stumble around chasing Mason and Schultz in much the same fashion as they stumble through *Hogan's Heroes*. Crane plays his character as a slightly sleazier version of Hogan, while the other three *Hogan's Heroes* cast members maintain the exact same accents and affects in the film as in the series.

Hogan's Heroes continues to influence the cinema. Two films of the past decade suggest, in one case, an interest in the series per se and, in the other, a continued engagement in the kind of cartoon historical fantasy of which it was a leading purveyor. Paul Schrader's biopic of Robert Crane, *Auto Focus* (2002), reveals *Hogan's Heroes*' leading man as someone torn between his allegiance to conservative postwar American values and the tremendous sexual freedoms that his success on the series afforded him. Crane, whose murder in 1978 remains unsolved, is depicted as a porn addict, whose wild sexual appetite and obsession with early video technology cost him his career and eventually his life.

Upon its premiere at Cannes in May 2009, critics immediately compared Tarantino's *Inglourious Basterds* to *Hogan's Heroes* and *The Dirty Dozen*. In Tarantino's film, a band of Jewish renegade Allied soldiers roam about the wartime French countryside butchering any members of the Wehrmacht they can find. In the end, they become part of a larger scheme to blow up a Parisian cinema at which the entire German high command is attending a film premiere. In this scenario, a small band of unorthodox soldiers manages to assassinate Hitler, Goebbels, and the rest of the key Nazi leaders, presumably bringing an end to the war as a whole. *Inglourious Basterds* shares with *Hogan's Heroes* the little man view of history in which the actions and inactions of small players, such as the German colonel Hans Landa (Christoph Waltz), Aldo Raines (Brad Pitt), or the Jewish cinema owner, Shosanna Dreyfus, do more to terminate the war than Eisenhower's D-day strategies or Patton's army. Whereas *Hogan's Heroes* rewrites history by suggesting that its main characters played a part in the backstory of what the average person knows about that history, Tarantino bends history to match his fantasy.

As I have demonstrated in this chapter, *Hogan's Heroes* and its cinematic cousins do little to further our understanding of World War II history. In fact, the series, which renders Germans of the Nazi era as either harmless or resistant to the regime and leaves the National Socialists' brutal crimes unmentioned, does active harm to a full accounting of the past. Even Tarantino's humorous historical fantasy forefronts the horrors of the Holocaust. The difference is, of course, that Tarantino's narrative is in the position to incorporate, albeit strangely, the discourse on the history and memory of the Holocaust that emerges after *Hogan's Heroes*.

I am left with the question of what relationship, if any, *Hogan's Heroes* has to empirical reality. The series' relationship to its historical setting is often little more than a cartoon prop. But its various strategies to stay relevant during the tumultuous period of its initial network run shed light on a different history with which the series engaged. In what follows I will turn to episodes of *Hogan's Heroes* to investigate what currents of contemporary culture it draws from to create its situational humor. In doing so, one will discover a television series far more engaged in its contemporary cultural and political conversations about militarization, Vietnam, and the Cold War than that for which its popular reception has given *Hogan's Heroes* credit.

Hogan's Heroes and Generational Change

In their book on Hollywood blacklisting and the television industry, Paul Buhle and David Wagner note the following of the *Hogan's Heroes* writing staff: "One of the industry's inside jokes was the antiwar, liberal, and left-wing character of the series' writing staff and most of its actors. . . . Dick Powell, none other than the former president of the banished Television Writers of America [a short-lived, leftist alternative union movement to the Screen Writers Guild, which had succumbed to HUAC pressure], was the lead writer who enjoyed the semi-sweet revenge of lambasting authority."[1] Buhle and Wagner's comments, however brief, remain among the very few acknowledgments that *Hogan's Heroes* may have been up to something other than puerile comedy. They suggest the series became an outlet for writers' frustrations regarding an environment in Southern California from the early 1950s through the mid-1960s that often excluded or punished dissidence. In this chapter I will undertake readings of episodes in the series to demonstrate that *Hogan's Heroes* uses the façade of iconic representation of World War II to engage in running commentary about the American involvement in Vietnam. I will follow the series' use of a variety of plot devices to offer a take on current events that was vague and general enough not to play as overly controversial, yet direct enough that a contemporary viewer who had watched Walter Cronkite on the CBS Evening News an hour before could have understood its implications. As such, *Hogan's Heroes* offers a compelling example of how the television industry of the late 1960s responded to competing pressures to be both relevant and commercially viable.

A sitcom trying not to be too topical would have had considerable difficulty keeping the events of the late 1960s from seeping into its episodes. It is the age not only of Vietnam but also of the Beatles, the rise of the hippie generation, the assassinations of Martin Luther King and Bobby Kennedy, the Apollo moon landing, and Woodstock. As *Hogan's Heroes* approached its 100th episode milestone, the show's producers understood that it had a future in the boom market of strip syndication— that is, the practice of running what were weekly shows in their network run on a daily schedule. Jack Gould of the *New York Times* describes aptly the experience of producers attempting to construct a series viable for syndication: "Because of the importance of replays over several years after a show's initial presentation, the situation comedy is confined to themes that will not become dated. All possibility of topicality is thereby instantly lost and the situation comedy must operate in the never-never land of enduring blandness and irrelevance to today's immediate world."[2] Faced with the contradictory demands to be both relevant and timeless, *Hogan's Heroes*' writers would need to become adept at a combination of ideological subtlety and broad humor.

I argued in chapter 2 that despite its setting *Hogan's Heroes* elides what was distinctive of World War II. I will contend in this chapter that *Hogan's Heroes*, as the only uniform comedy to run during the length of the major American intervention in Vietnam, presents a commentary about war that is more frequently a reaction to the war in Southeast Asia than the previous one in Europe. The series animates the cultural attitudes about the military, war, and authoritarianism as they shifted wildly in the late 1960s.

While critics of the series have most frequently attacked the central premise of making a comedy set in a German POW camp, I have argued that the critical unit of study in this case is not the series as a whole but the individual episode. Even Gould, who dismissed the series when it premiered, revisited his opinion two years later noting, "The idea of making sport of the Nazis as clownish oafs originally struck this corner as a wildly improbable premise, but the continued run of Edward H. Feldman's production speaks for itself."[3] Gould goes on to suggest that *Hogan's Heroes* overcomes its ridiculous setup through "adroit use of setting and plot."[4] He seems also to appreciate the function of the series at the level of the episode.

Of course, since I cannot perform a careful analysis of each of the 168 installments of the series, I must establish some criteria by which to decide which episodes to sample. I have chosen episodes from each season. Each episode contains one of the main storylines often repeated in the series, such as the threat that either Klink or Schultz will be sent to the Russian front. I will look to these episodes for exhibitions of knowledge and cultural assumptions that circulated at the time of their production and then work through the series thematically, being careful to sample episodes from each season so as to attend to change over the run of the series. I run the danger of a confirmation bias if I simply pick out those installments that directly address sociopolitical concerns of the day and then claim that they represent the whole of the series. But I am making a more modest claim, one that insists only that topical concerns were a significant part of *Hogan's Heroes*' storyline. Moreover, I will show that the series is not static over time but rather displays subtle yet important shifts in attitude and emphasis, shifts that stem from a constant mining of the cultural terrain on the part of the series' writers.

I will begin with a survey of episodes that differentiate Hogan and his band from the version of the World War II combatant as hero. Although the title might suggest something grander, the "heroism" for which the POWs are credited often consists of trickery. Moreover, a picture of the World War II soldier as a morally complicated subject gradually replaces the one of the hero. From there I will move on to the depictions of military authority in the series. One of the tendencies to work its way through Western popular cultural in the course of the late 1960s was antiauthoritarianism. Whether it was through the Oedipal gestures of generational conflict, the direct protests against the Vietnam War, or the myriad shifts in moral and aesthetic values that emerged in that time period, a general societal attitude of "sticking it to the man" was in play. As we follow *Hogan's Heroes*' antiauthoritarian story lines from season to season, we will see that they shift in ways that sometimes mirror the sociopolitical terrain and sometimes deviate from it.

Perhaps the greatest attitudinal repositioning that occurred during the run of the series was that toward the U.S. military and its involvement abroad. Many of the episodes, including some described below, thematize the normalization of guerilla warfare, sympathy with the enemy, the tenuousness of military alliances, and the violation of the rules of warfare. While the German generals are always the brunt of the series' humor, the various stunts pulled at their expense change in nature over time. Moreover, the German brass is not the only officer class that comes in for lampooning.

The Cold War, of which the war in Vietnam was a front, emerges in *Hogan's Heroes* in a variety of ways. Occasional Russian characters appear in the series, the most frequent being the recurring character Marya, a Russian spy working with Hogan. The Russian front serves a dual purpose in *Hogan's Heroes*. The threat of being sent there animates both the Cold War themes and another ongoing response to the military culture of the era—namely, draft dodging. Throughout the run of the series

General Burkhalter (Leon Askin) yet again receives bad war news. ("Some of Their Planes Are Missing," September 16, 1967)

the theme of preventing one or another of the characters from actually having to go to war motivates episodes.

Uniformed Buffoons

Hogan's Heroes is a generic hybrid of a military comedy and a spy comedy. It upholds the various power relations that are generally used as the sources of humor in military comedy, often lampooning the officer class as a whole while retaining solidarity with the officer who is central to the cast of characters. This is made convenient in *Hogan's Heroes* by Hogan being generally the only Allied officer around. Hogan shows next to no deference toward the high-ranking Germans whom he encounters in each episode. Establishing the buffoonery of the German officers is made easier by their being dressed in (an often exaggerated version of) the enemy uniform. The military comedy conceit is extended further in Hogan's relationship with Klink. They are equal in rank, although both acknowledge that Hogan is superior in talent. While their power relationship is structurally controlled by the fact that Klink runs the prison in which Hogan is supposedly incarcerated, nobody, not even Klink, seems to operate as if that defines their relationship. Hogan's use of Klink's ineptitude and his own sovereignty in camp matters offer another source of comedic conflict. As such, the show does not differ tremendously from the premise of *Gomer Pyle, U.S.M.C.*, which I mentioned in chapter 1. While the viewer knows that the drill sergeant, Carter, is in charge of Pyle and his buddies, almost every episode revolves around Pyle proving how much Carter actually relies on him.

Once Hogan and his fellow saboteurs embark on their missions, the combination of spoof spy thriller and comedy found in *Get Smart* offers a better generic comparison. *Hogan's Heroes* emphasizes its generic debt to the spy thriller genre musically by scoring all of the caper scenes with a percussive soundtrack similar to those found in Bond films as well as *I Spy*, *Get Smart*, and *The Man from U.N.C.L.E.* The series works to make it clear that the prisoners are spies and saboteurs, not combatants; that is to say, while they are nominally still in the military, they are doing intelligence work. Hogan's unit specializes in sabotage, information gathering, and escape rather than combat.

This distinction becomes important when one notes who is portrayed as belonging to the military. The Germans are shown almost always in their formal uniforms. This is most peculiar with the Gestapo agents, who are mostly shown in their militaristic parade uniforms rather than the civilian clothes that were more common for that unit day to day. This costuming choice enhances the image of the Germans as the militaristic culture in contrast to the informal fatigues of the prisoners. Because the prisoners are from different countries or different branches of the U.S. military, their uniforms offer little uniformity. Hogan, the only authority figure among the prisoners, always appears in a pressed officer's shirt, leather flyer's jacket, and officer's cap. While the uniform is enough to distinguish him among prisoners, in comparison to the Germans he looks more like the leader of a motorcycle gang—indeed, like Marlon Brando in *The Wild One* (Lazlo Benedek, 1953)—than an officer of equal rank to his captor, Klink. Since the series, even here, makes no attempt at authenticity, the uniforms are designed to set the Germans up for the antiauthoritarian fall that each episode constructs. When the prisoners themselves don German uniforms it is always accompanied by a laugh track.

Obviously, the same antiauthoritarian attitude directed toward the Germans could also be deployed against Hogan as the ranking officer among the POWs. The only sign of such insurrection in the first season comes in an episode titled "I Look Better in Basic Black" (April 1, 1966). In this episode, the first of many that involves cross-dressing, Newkirk and LeBeau resist Hogan's command that they dress in ladies' apparel to aid an escape. Early in the episode, Newkirk makes a series of comments reflecting resentment toward the officer class. When Newkirk threatens mutiny rather than consent to cross-dressing, Hogan asserts his authority and yet ameliorates that conflict by donning a skirt and wig himself. In general Hogan's authority remains unquestioned throughout the series. Yet he is mindful of the Geneva Conventions when he reminds his troops that he cannot command them to take the actions he is asking of them. His authority is grounded more in his character and his relationships with the other prisoners than his rank. More than once, the men's use of uniforms as disguises for a spy mission causes Hogan to be outranked by another prisoner, which in turn provides fodder for the laugh track. Stripes on a uniform do not justify respect. Carter outranks LeBeau and Newkirk, yet he is most often the brunt of jokes about his intelligence and abilities.

All Quiet on the Russian Front:
Hogan's Heroes and Draft Dodging

By the time the second season of *Hogan's Heroes* began filming in the summer of 1966 the United States was fully committed in Vietnam. After numerous attempts to overwhelm the Vietcong forces with large numbers of American troops, U.S. commanders were beginning to understand that they were engaged in a different type of war, one for which their training was not quite suited. Despite numerous large deployments, the Americans and South Vietnamese continually failed to engage similarly large Vietcong forces. What the Johnson administration had claimed would be a brief and successful military campaign was turning into a much lengthier commitment that was beginning to lose support both domestically and abroad.

Hogan, LeBeau, and Newkirk suit up for another mission. ("I Look Better in Basic Black," April 1, 1966)

While the Americans were experiencing frustration fighting against a combination insurgent and guerilla war in Vietnam, the war sitcom was making light of a similar frustration on the part of Germans on prime-time Saturday night. A reading of the series as equating the Pentagon with the World War II German military brass would certainly be a stretch; yet, *Hogan's Heroes* does draw increasingly frequent parallels between the two military apparatuses. Whether or not the show's writers intended these parallels (and there is plenty of reason to believe they did), a late 1960s television audience would have been sensitized to notice them. Moreover, *Hogan's Heroes* clears room, not only for a discussion of insurgent warfare, but also for imagining choosing not to fight.

The second season of *Hogan's Heroes* offers the first of many episodes in which the topic is the pending transfer of either Klink or Schultz to the Russian front. This conceit allows the episode to mine a number of issues in the cultural terrain at once. In "Don't Forget to Write" (December 9, 1966), Klink is trapped into volunteering for duty on the German eastern front. Given both the high casualty rate and the frozen conditions, the transfer to Russia is always treated as a likely fatal move. Believing that the retention of the incompetent camp commandant is crucial for the preservation of their underground operations, the prisoners endeavor to help Klink avoid combat duty.

Act 1 of "Don't Forget to Write" comprises a draft-dodging narrative in which the prisoners attempt to keep Klink from passing his physical examination. Hogan's suggestion of a way to beat the draft reveals the methods as common knowledge:

> Hogan: Of course, there are ways. But that wouldn't interest you. Well, tally ho! Go get'm!
>
> Klink: Hogan, wait a minute! What do you mean? Wait!
>
> Hogan: Not passing the physical. Getting yourself into a weakened condition. Starving yourself. Catching a cold. Maybe even pneumonia, if you're lucky. It's been

done before.

Klink: Hogan, I am a German and an officer! Now, what you are suggesting is obviously dishonest, vile, and deceitful. (*Laugh track.*) Now, if I am ordered to the Russian front to be shot out of the wild blue yonder and die in the snow, it is what I must do. (*Laugh track.*)

Hogan: Spoken like a true German patriot. (*Laugh track.*)

Klink: Thank You. (*Laugh track.*)

Hogan: Good Luck! Don't forget to write. (*Laugh track as Hogan leaves Klink's office and shuts the door.*)

Klink: (*No laugh track. Klink proudly walks back toward his desk, sits down, pauses and then . . .*) Hogan! Wait! (*Laugh track.*)

84

The placement of the laugh track alone suggests that Klink's patriotic speech is to be understood as ridiculous. When he inevitably agrees to the plan, Schultz and the POWs team up to put Klink on a starvation diet, make him susceptible to pneumonia, and deprive him of sleep, all in the service of both deteriorating his condition and humiliating him. While attempting to keep him awake, Carter recounts how his friend Charlie attempted to hide underneath a porch from the American draft board. Act 2 begins with all of their efforts coming to naught as the doctor informs Klink that only death would keep him from qualifying physically for service on the Russian front. Thus, the prisoners must concoct a different method to save Klink. They must prove to Burkhalter that Klink's replacement, Captain Gruber, would, in fact, do a worse job than Klink.

Service avoidance comes up again later the same season in "The Swing Shift" (February 3, 1967). The storyline consists of the regular industrial espionage conceit found in dozens of episodes. The POWs' tricks result in Newkirk first becoming foreman of a munitions plant and then being conscripted into the German army. Again, Newkirk feigns an array of ailments from deafness to fainting spells in order to flunk his physical. Again, the doctor claims that being alive is about all the fitness the army requires. As in "Don't Forget to Write," the draft-dodging schemes fail while claims to competence in some other part of the war effort, this time Newkirk's role as foreman, prevent his conscription.

"The Swing Shift" is noteworthy in one other regard—namely, its attitude toward the military-industrial complex. The factory that the POWs intend to sabotage has been converted from auto to cannon manufacturing. When Klink expresses dismay to Burkhalter at the loss of car production, the latter blurts out, "Cannons, cannons, cannons, cannons . . . that's what we're making now, cannons!" Though intended in the story to express support for the war effort, Askin delivers the lines in a way that ridicules the war machine.

Hogan's Heroes is at times rather masterful at deploying signifiers from World War II in a way that is more suggestive of Vietnam-era signification. No episode epitomizes this tendency more than episode 60, "Colonel Klink's Secret Weapon" (March 24, 1967). The installment itself depicts the prisoners, as well as Klink and Schultz, as suffering under a new camp discipline regime enforced by the well-connected Sergeant Frank. In this episode, the differentiation between the POWs and the Germans breaks down as both sets of protagonists fall under Frank's self-righteous command. Military discipline procedures are lampooned as arbitrary and nonsensical. Moreover, they threaten Hogan's operation, which depends on German inefficiency. As is predictable in the series, Hogan concocts a way to humiliate and discredit Frank. Under the watchful eye of the inspector general, who has come to camp to assess efficiency, Sergeant Frank's uniform comes apart at the seams, leaving him wearing nothing but underclothes decorated with a victory/peace sign—that is, a sketch of a hand raising the index and middle fingers in the shape of a V. Read in terms of World War II, this would be seen as Churchill's famous victory hand gesture. But in terms of the mid- to late 1960s, the gesture had been co-opted into war protestors' call for peace. In fact, in March 1967 when the episode aired, the latter iteration of the gesture was more likely to have been recognized. A soldier is depicted flashing a peace symbol during a prime-time sitcom.

In the fall of 1967, *Hogan's Heroes* moved from Friday to Saturday night, where it was sandwiched between *My Three Sons* and *Petticoat Junction* and appeared opposite NBC's *Saturday Night at the Movies*. Thus, it was no longer in a time slot in which it competed against the more politically charged spy thrillers, such as *The Man from U.N.C.L.E.* Yet, the episodes of the third season of *Hogan's Heroes* draw attention to the political issues of the day more so than at any other period of the show's run. By 1967, war, labor, and civil rights protests were erupting all across the country. Six months before he declined to run for

Hogan's Heroes calls for peace ("Colonel Klink's Secret Weapon," March 24, 1967)

a second full term, Lyndon Johnson had lost control of his public image as a war president and his generals could not make a convincing public case that they had a workable strategy for the war. Under these conditions the *Hogan's Heroes* episode "Is General Hammerschlag Burning?" aired on November 18. Having already discussed the racial politics of the episode in chapter 1, here I will note that the episode suggests a shift in attitude, or at least expression, among the series' writers as it engages much more directly the political mood of the time.

The setup of the episode itself is compelling when read against the backdrop of the day. At a time when Johnson and the U.S. war effort in Vietnam were under severe international criticism for the indiscriminate destruction of North Vietnamese cities, "Is General Hammerschlag Burning?" starts with Hogan being asked to interfere in the Germans' desire to destroy Paris if they are forced to vacate. Thus Hogan and Kinch become directly involved in undermining the German military machine's plans to commit mass destruction not unlike that which was being reported on the nightly news.

As with every episode of *Hogan's Heroes*, this one looks like little more than a wacky caper. But a contemporary television viewer would not have had difficulty connecting the frustrations of the U.S. war effort to those of the general in this episode. First it presents a war leader as absolutely helpless in the martial task with which he is faced. His military plans become the episode's object of derision. Given his pending failure, he plans massive urban destruction as an act of desperation, not as a strategy for victory. Moreover, when Hogan is impersonating a medium, he mouths the late general Otto von Bismarck decrying the competence of the generals.

The Entangled Alliance

Given its Cold War context, one of the trickier narrative challenges of the series lies in the portrayal of the various Russian characters who enter the camp. As I have mentioned, while the pilot episode included a Russian among Hogan's band of men, when Leonid Kinsky chose to leave the cast, the role was simply cut rather than filled with another actor. This leads one to wonder whether the creators had second thoughts about including a Russian in their Allied POW family. Representing Russians at all sympathetically at the height of the Cold War carried political pitfalls. The most frequent appearance of a Russian came with the recurring role of Marya, a Russian spy who generally consorts with German generals. Marya and Hogan's relationship is marked both by strong sexual tension and a high level of mutual distrust. Hogan is always half-expecting Marya to betray him, but Marya is also the only regularly appearing character in the series whose tactical intelligence can match Hogan's.

Marya is first introduced in the second season as part of an effort to inject more salaciousness into the storyline. "A Tiger Hunt in Paris" (November 18 and 25, 1966) is a rare double episode. In it another Hogan love interest and fellow spy, Tiger, has been captured in Paris and is about to be transferred to Gestapo headquarters in Berlin for questioning. Marya is identified early on as a White Russian and thus supposedly anti-Bolshevik, though that trait is never again pursued. More importantly, the question of her trustworthiness and loyalties arises almost immediately. When pressed as to why Hogan should provide her with vital information, Marya notes that they are "more or less on the same side." She then clarifies the statement further: "More on the same side so that we can work together from time to time, just enough less that I would like the information." As in all subsequent episodes, Marya proves to be at once dangerous and reliable. Her flirtation with LeBeau keeps the Frenchman convinced of her loyalty, despite all evidence to the contrary, thus giving a nod to the widely held Cold War belief that France was often playing both sides against the middle.

The Marya episodes required some of the most complicated narration in the entire series. Nita Talbot, who was nominated for an Emmy for her portrayal of the Russian spy, displays at once flawless timing and excessively accented English in her Marya performances. The episodes always require one more level of suspense to accommodate the multiple layers of deception necessary to bring the plot to a happy conclusion. Just when Hogan is finally sure that she has sold him out, she carries out a plan that results in far greater destruction or deception than Hogan and his men would have been able to achieve without her. Thus, with its most frequent reference to the complicated relationship between Russia and the rest of the Allied forces, *Hogan's Heroes* constructs a view of the Soviets that is much more aligned with the attitudes during World War II than with those that developed in the subsequent decades. The viewer and Hogan both know that this is not an allegiance but a contingent working arrangement, one that is always likely to break down.

In episode 77, "The Hostage" (December 16, 1967), Marya has attached herself to a General von Heiner, who wants to find out what lies behind a rash of sabotage incidents in the area. Upon being tipped off by Marya, von Heiner lays a trap for Hogan, telling him about a fuel depot located nearby (about which Hogan already knows). When Hogan tries to find out why Marya has betrayed the prisoners, she simply assures him that her relationship with "Bobo" von Heiner is all part of a plan that Hogan should trust. Convinced that he is doomed either way, Hogan plants a bomb to blow up the fuel depot. Thereafter, at Marya's suggestion, Hogan is taken hostage at the fuel depot. Marya visits him and convinces him to tell "Bobo" of his plans. Hogan offers a fake plan to the general and is sent away with Marya just before the depot and von Heiner are blown up. Celebrating another successful caper, Marya exclaims:

> Beautiful, Hogan! Oh, you're a fun person!
> Hogan: Why did you make it so hard for me? Why didn't you work with me instead of against me?

Marya: Who cares about the rocket fuel! They're not bombing Moscow with their rockets, just London. (*Laugh track.*)

Hogan: Then what were you after?

Marya: We cannot trust Hitler to shoot all his own generals. Some we have to take care of them ourselves. (*Laugh track.*)

Hogan: Oh, Bobo!

Marya: Oh, I am desolate. . . . Will you kiss me now or later? (*Laugh track.*)

Hogan: I think I will make it later.

Marya: Shy, desperately shy! (*She kisses him during laugh track.*)

90

Marya reveals that hers is a parallel and compatible mission to the one into which she has tricked Hogan and his Western Allied prisoners. Yet she remains throughout the run a seductive and dangerous ally.

A few weeks after "The Hostage" aired "Two Nazis for the Price of One" (December 30, 1967) gives us a picture of how a plotline about World War II intrigue could easily morph into one about Cold War espionage. In the episode a high-ranking SS officer, Gruppenführer Freitag, has heard tell of the American Manhattan Project and wants to know more about it from Hogan. Hogan has no knowledge of the project but understands that it must be important. He also realizes that Freitag knows more than he should and will have to be eliminated. The episode begins with the kind of irreverence toward the crimes of German history for which the series became famous:

(*Klink and Hochstetter are in Klink's office, Hogan enters.*)

Hogan: You wanted to see me, Colonel? . . . Oh, I didn't realize you had company.

Hochstetter: The Gestapo is not company.

Russian spy, Marya (Nita Talbot), tries to convince Hogan to trust her. ("The Hostage," December 16, 1967)

Hogan: Frankly, I never thought much of them myself. (*Laugh track.*)

Klink: Hogan, you will show a little respect for Major Hochstetter.

Hogan: Just a little, sir? (*Laugh track.*)

Klink: I mean a lot of . . . please, don't twist my words . . .

Hochstetter: Tell me, Hogan, what do you know about the Manhattan Project? What is it?

Hogan: Maybe they are selling the island back to the Indians?

Hochstetter: The 504th bomb group was assigned to the Manhattan Project, is that right?

Hogan: Were they?

Hochstetter: You should know. You commanded the 504th bomb group.

Hogan: Did I?

When Hogan resists Hochstetter's attempts at interrogation, the latter leans on Hogan with the SS's reputation for torture.

Hochstetter: Of course, we could give you the time to think it over in a special cell we have. It is not big enough to stand up in and it is not big enough to lie down in.

Hogan: Sounds like a hotel room I once had in Cleveland. (*Laugh track.*)

Hochstetter: During the day the temperature is 140 degrees and at night it is below freezing.

Hogan: That's the hotel all right! (*Laugh track.*)

Hochstetter: Then if you don't talk, you will be starved, tortured, and shot. Well, Hogan, what do you say?

Hogan: What can I say? You've made me homesick for Cleveland. (*Laugh track.*)

The exchange reinforces both the lampooning attitude toward the criminal aspects of the Nazi war machine as well as the deadpan humor that permeates the series' dialogue. It also sets up the double spy narrative that will follow. Hogan realizes not only that the Germans have found out about a top secret American mission but to have done so they must also have a spy placed high up in the command structure. The task of preventing the SS from finding out more about the secret American nuclear program is much more of a Cold War plot than a World War II one.

Fearing that they have been compromised, the prisoners all prepare to disband their operation and flee to England. But before they leave, Hogan decides that he must eliminate Freitag. It is the only episode in which Hogan or the others attempt a direct assassination. Normally, if a character must die, they simply cause him to be in harm's way. As Hogan enters Klink's office he hears a shot. Freitag's lieutenant, Mannheim, resentful of having been treated shabbily by his superior officer, has beaten Hogan to the punch and shot him through the window. Mannheim then storms into the office to finish the job, whereupon he stumbles across Klink, Hogan, and Schultz. The latter conveniently loses his weapon at the moment he is asked to use it.

Hogan's Heroes' most convincing addition to the Cold War narrative comes in its formal construction. The very mix of military comedy façade with a spy narrative pits Hogan's modern techniques of espionage and sabotage—that is, the nonmilitaristic interventions of the Cold War—against a bloated military machine, the mechanism of the last war. Hogan and his men apply their trickery to prevent the Germans from gaining technological or material advantage rather than engaging in direct battles. Thus, it is Hogan who is fighting a Cold War while his adversaries are mired in a troop-based conflict.

The tension among the Allies provides the framework for "A Russian Is Coming," which aired originally on November 25, 1967, a week after "Is General Hammerschlag Burning?" In this episode, the POWs are hiding a downed Soviet pilot, Igor Piotkin (Bob Hastings), who provides comic shtick through his distrust of his fellow prisoners. Piotkin insists that Hogan return him to the Soviet Union rather than the usual escape route to England. Hogan then concocts a plan whereby Piotkin is dressed up as a German lieutenant who is to be sent to the Russian front. The Russian is portrayed as an ideological buffoon who talks about grain production and "the fulfillment of the five year plan." The interaction between Piotkin and the Western POWs leaves both sides wondering why it is that they are meant to be allies. The episode ends with Hogan musing, "Wouldn't it be funny if he really wanted to go to the Russian front." The joke does not refer only to the caper that the prisoners have just pulled off. It suggests a general ridiculousness on the part of anyone who would voluntarily go to war. Moreover, although Germany is at war with all of the Allies, the diegetic military confrontation that is always mentioned is with the Russians.

Quagmire

The fourth season of *Hogan's Heroes* began with a world in much more turmoil than it had been a season earlier. The Tet Offensive and American inability to make progress in Vietnam led esteemed CBS anchorman Walter Cronkite to say, "We are mired in a stalemate." As a result of collapsing public support for the war, Johnson chose not to seek reelection. The assassinations of Martin Luther King Jr. and Robert F. Kennedy had left the American political world in turmoil. Antiwar and student protests destabilized regimes all over the world.

Judged by the level of political engagement both before and after the season that began in September 1968, the writers kept most of the episodes of that fourth season remarkably neutral. This could have been due to the tremendous turmoil at CBS over another hit show, *The Smothers Brothers Comedy Hour*, which was under constant surveillance by the network over its topically political content. Though the underlying antimilitarism of mocking uniformed (German) authority and the general suggestion that the military brass is filled with incompetent nincompoops pervades each episode, the plotlines themselves are generally formulaic. Given the widespread political turmoil of that year, it might not be that surprising that the writers for *Hogan's Heroes* chose to keep their heads down. However, the first episode of the 1968–69 season, "Clearance Sale at the Black Market" (September 28, 1968), is rather remarkable. In this installment, the prisoners are using Schultz (more precisely his wide girth) to transfer messages to and from the underground agents in town. The notes are surreptitiously placed in

Schultz's belt, which Schultz's girlfriend at the local bar removes during their embraces. The episode's humor derives from the notion that someone would be attracted to the rotund sergeant. When Schultz mistakenly witnesses a black market transaction in progress between a local saloonkeeper and a Gestapo agent, the Gestapo quickly arranges for Schultz to be transferred to the Russian front, thereby injecting into the episode another draft-dodging narrative.

The scene begins with an establishing shot of Schultz entering Klink's quarters, where the latter is sitting and eating. Klink offers Schultz a drink and refers to him as "my boy," thereby raising Schultz's suspicion:

> Klink: Schultz, I have the pleasure to tell you that you are being transferred to the Eastern front. (*Cut to a shot of Schultz with a quizzical look. Laugh track. Schultz takes a drink straight from the schnapps bottle.*) Isn't that thrilling news!
>
> Schultz: Thrilling? I'm out of my mind. (*Laugh track.*) What happened, Herr Kommandant? Did I do something wrong?
>
> Klink: Of course not! You are just being asked to use your knowledge and experience in the service of the Third Reich.
>
> Schultz: Yeah?
>
> Klink: You want Germany to win the war, don't you?
>
> Schultz: (*Noncommittally.*) Yeah.
>
> Klink: Being transferred to the Eastern front, you can make that possible.
>
> Schultz: Would it be so bad if we *lost* the war? (*Laugh track.*)
>
> Klink: Schultz, we are going to miss your sense of humor around here.
>
> Schultz: Herr Kommandant, I have flat feet. I am overweight. My eyes are bad. And, I am not so young any-

more.

Klink: Oh, that doesn't matter.

Schultz: How about dandruff? (*Laugh track.*)

Klink: Come on, Schultz.

Schultz: I also have nervousness. (*Laugh track.*)

Klink: You, nervous? Don't be silly.

Schultz: I'm silly too! (*Laugh track.*)

Klink: I think at this point you would find almost anything wrong with yourself.

Schultz: Try me! (*Laugh track.*)

Klink: Well, I realize you are not exactly what we would call a perfect physical specimen . . .

Schultz: Now, you are on the right track. (*Laugh track.*)

Klink: But you have something much more important than physical perfection. You have a fighting spirit.

Schultz: I'll get rid of it. (*Laugh track.*)

Klink: In these times, my boy, a man in uniform has two choices: either he fights, or he is called a coward.

Schultz: I'd rather be a coward. (*Light laugh track.*)

Klink: Do you want to give up the chance for greater glory on the battlefield? Do you want to go on being called a coward?

Schultz: Why not? That's something I understand. (*Light laugh track.*)

Schultz's quizzical, almost indifferent look when Klink asks him whether or not he wants Germany to win the war, as well as his query about whether or not it would be so bad if they lost, is this bit of dialogue's most direct engagement with the public discourse of the time. Moreover, the audience is sutured into Schultz's point of view through the insertion of the laugh track after each of his excuses for why he should not be sent into combat.

Walter Cronkite's quagmire comments in February 1968 also expressed pessimism about the potential for victory or

Schultz tries to avoid the Russian front. ("Clearance Sale at the Black Market," September 28, 1968)

defeat in Vietnam to Americans, thus instigating considerable public and private debate about the war. The troubles in Southeast Asia were at the forefront of the tight presidential campaign between Hubert H. Humphrey and Richard Nixon that was being waged when the episode aired. Anybody who had watched the evening news an hour before *Hogan's Heroes* came on would have had no trouble assimilating Schultz's query about the consequences of losing the war with the discussions of Vietnam in the news. Moreover, it is noteworthy that Klink finds humor in his sergeant's question rather than defending the war aims of the Third Reich. Wanting to win a war that was understood as unwinnable is the joke of this exchange.

The prisoners question the legitimacy of Schultz having been called up in the first place. Because he is such an unfit soldier, his being called to battle must be a sign of corruption somewhere, they surmise. Again, I could suggest an allegorical reading in which we substitute the Gestapo for the corrupt American military-industrial complex. I would rather note that a superficial reading of Schultz's reaction to the war does everything that needs to be done. Schultz expresses clear indifference to the outcome of the war and his own participation in it. The POWs side with him and expose the Gestapo agent's black market profiteering operation. *Hogan's Heroes* allows the viewer to root for the guy who is trying to avoid the war and mock those who believe in the war effort. Moreover, the show suggests that the continuance of the war is inherently corrupt. This is, of course, all done in the disguise of World War II uniforms.

In a season where the series displayed a cautious approach to the empirical world, "Clearance Sale at the Black Market" reflects that caution topically and displays a certain political charisma at the level of dialogue. The same can be said generally about the fourth season in which writers seem unwilling to reveal their critical hand too openly. While far from underground humor, season 4 of *Hogan's Heroes* still feeds off of popular sentiments about war, military service, and the competence of the military brass.

The recurring guest appearances of Bernard Fox as Colonel Crittendon provided *Hogan's Heroes*' writers another opportunity to develop storylines to mine cultural attitudes about, among other things, military rank and ceremony. Crittendon, the bumbling member of the Royal Air Force who outranks Hogan by a technicality, is the Allied version of Klink. The technical outranking is an important plot device, because it forces Hogan and his men into idiotic adventures concocted by the inept and incorrigible colonel. Moreover, Crittendon's arrival in the series' fifth episode, "The Flight of the Valkyrie" (October 15, 1966), allows writers to introduce a number of factors into the plot mix that will remain throughout the series.

Even the Allies have nitwit officers (Bernard Fox as Colonel Crittendon). ("Crittendon's Commandos," March 20, 1970)

Most important, "The Flight of the Valkyrie" creates a scenario in which Crittendon stipulates that he is a soldier, not a spy. He insists that a soldier's first duty is to escape and rejoin his unit. Indeed, when Hogan asks "hypothetically" what he would say were a sabotage ring being run out of a prison camp, Crittendon insists that the Geneva Conventions and his honor as a soldier would require him to turn the saboteurs over to the Germans. Here, as well as at other points, the series admits that the heroic escapades of Hogan and his band were technically criminal and, were they caught, the Geneva Conventions—to which Hogan frequently appeals in disputes with Klink—would license their execution. But Crittendon's desire to return to combat is what sets him up as the idiot, whereas Hogan's abilities as a spy are what make him the smart one.

By the fifth season of *Hogan's Heroes*, from 1969 to 1970, the idea of combat avoidance was so well established that its necessity literally goes without saying. In episode 141, "The Sergeant's Analyst" (March 6, 1970), Schultz is caught sleeping on the job by Burkhalter and punished by being ordered to the Russian front. Without consulting Schultz and without discussing it with the other prisoners, Hogan immediately begins to scheme to have the order reversed. His plan involves convincing Burkhalter that Schultz is still useful to the camp, primarily by bribing the general with goods he finds in the prisoners' barracks. This only reinforces the broader sociological suspicion that one could buy oneself out of military service.

Hogan's Heroes limped through its last season, moving from Friday to Sunday evening and carrying on with the loss of Ivan Dixon as Sergeant Kinchloe.[5] In 1969 *Hogan's Heroes* moved from its long-held position on Saturday night to the Friday night lineup. The heavily scripted banter that carried the show for the first five years became thinner. More airtime was spent with the combination of slapstick and suspense that had always been a lesser part of the episode mix. Nonetheless, the irreverent attitude projected by the series in previous seasons remained in place to the very end. "To Russia without Love" first aired on January 31, 1971, a little over two months before the series' first run ended. At the point when the episode was filmed, both CBS and Bing Crosby Productions were hinting that they wanted *Hogan's Heroes*' run to end. As Howard Caine put it, "In order to syndicate you needed at least five years in the can. . . . Unless a show was hugely successful they wanted to get it off the air as soon as possible because they made their big profit in syndication."[6]

Because the convention of the concluding episode was not established when *Hogan's Heroes* wound down, "To Russia without Love" is as useful as any episode of the final season from which to draw conclusions about how the series engaged with its moment. The episode narrates the visit of a Luftwaffe officer,

Colonel Becker, from the Russian front. Becker seeks Hogan's help in getting transferred to Klink's post at Stalag 13. In return, Becker promises to provide Hogan with the Germans' plans for a counteroffensive in Stalingrad. To facilitate the switch, Hogan sets out to convince Klink that Stalingrad is not the hell that everyone claims it is. Hogan enlists a beautiful underground agent to convince Klink that the real reason officers tell such horrible stories about the eastern front is that it is actually a den of iniquity that they want to keep for their own enjoyment. She reels off a list of the names of the corrupt generals. It is noteworthy that the writers include a "General Kissinger," which is hard to interpret as anything but a jab at Henry Kissinger, who was at that moment national security advisor and one of the Nixon administration's chief defenders of the Vietnam War.

The agent convinces Klink that Becker, Kissinger, and the other officers are having such a lovely time that Klink insists on joining them. Klink then feigns competence as a ruthless soldier to convince Burkhalter to transfer him (and Schultz). Most of the laugh lines and shtick rest on Klink's expression (to Burkhalter) of his incomprehensible wish to be sent off to war. By 1971, as both *Hogan's Heroes* and the escalation in Vietnam are winding down, the idea that someone would willingly commit himself to combat in the "East" is nothing more than a joke. No further explanation is needed.

Hogan's Heroes as a series concludes on a much more melancholy note than it began. The last episode, "Rockets or Romance" (April 4, 1971), sets up a mission like dozens before it in which the prisoners are assigned to help locate German missiles that the Allied bombers have set out to destroy. Hogan is holed up in a cabin with Lily Frankel, yet another beautiful woman from the underground, thus setting up the usual combination of sexual innuendo and espionage work. When the mission finally succeeds, Frankel says, "It's nice, is it not, when the mission's accomplished." The pacing of the episode is noticeably slower than was usual for the series during its run.

It provides no epiphany sequence in which Hogan lays out the perfect plan. The mission seems like cleanup work. It appears that, despite the fact that the war shows no signs of concluding, Hogan and his men have only one final task. *Hogan's Heroes* ends with Klink, the bootlicking officer who has spent six seasons actively avoiding combat duty, setting loose a rocket that ends up destroying General Burkhalter's house.

*H*ogan's Heroes may have made no significant contribution to the understanding of the meaning of World War II. In fact, I have suggested it was counterproductive to such an understanding. The series preserves a moment before a more critical consciousness about the Holocaust and its moral significance had emerged among the larger public. But the series did engage, however indirectly, in a conversation about Vietnam. It lampoons old modes of warfare and a military apparatus that remains stuck in the past. To be sure, it does not rise to the level of urgency of the era's actual war protests. Rather, the series is one born of a more widely held anxiety about the Cold War. It insists that uniformed authority is laughable and newer forms of engagement are unsettling. Throughout the series, *Hogan's Heroes* suggests that, in warfare, the line between what is justified and what is criminal is not easily ascertained. Moreover, as in the Marya episodes, it insists the lines about who was friend and who was foe are blurry. In short, it offers a level of skepticism that was generally aligned with mainstream American attitudes as they developed throughout the six years of the series' run.

It is broadly accepted that Middle America in the late 1960s was conflicted about Vietnam. What I have tried to do here is insist that popular television did not wait until the era of "quality television"—that is, after the Vietnam war had slipped from the headlines—to weave it into sitcom narratives. Not only does *Hogan's Heroes* lampoon the notions of military service and strategy, it offers the far more troubling suggestion that military conflict is perpetual. All of this is done in the form of prime-time comedy that seems to have flown under the political radar. Far from a radical example of socially critical television, I offer *Hogan's Heroes* as a prime example of how commercial television was shaped by the tumultuous period in which it was made. Whether one is talking about *The Flintstones*, *The Andy Griffith Show*, *Gilligan's Island*, *All in the Family*, or *Hogan's Heroes*, any long-running television show must sift through the grains of its cultural context to find narrative material, attitudes, and commonly held values with which to make itself relevant. Rather than claiming more literacy or psychological depth for one type of program over another, one would do better to consider where each show invests itself and how it speaks to its moment. When we do that with Hogan, Klink, Schultz, and company, we find a show that taught America to laugh at our own martial foibles and political unease long before *M*A*S*H* taught us to cry about them.

Introduction

1. Stan Freberg, *It Only Hurts When I Laugh* (New York: Crown, 1988), 132.
2. Horace Newcomb, "Magnum: The Champagne of TV?" *Channels of Communication* 5, no. 1 (1985): 23–26.
3. Erik Barnouw, *Tube of Plenty: The Evolution of American Television*, 2nd rev.ed. (New York: Oxford University Press, 1992), 300.
4. Barnouw, *Tube of Plenty*, 376.
5. Max Horkheimer and Theodor W. Adorno, "Mass Culture as Mass Deception," in *The Dialectic of Enlightenment* (New York: Continuum, 1987), 120–67.
6. Jon Heitlang, *"The Man from U.N.C.L.E." Book: The Behind-the-Scenes Story of a Television Classic* (New York: St. Martin's Press, 1987), 49.
7. *Campo 44* never made it to production. For further information, see Brenda Scott Royce, *"Hogan's Heroes": Behind the Scenes at Stalag 13* (Los Angeles: Renaissance Books, 1998).
8. See Peter Hay, *Canned Laughter: The Best Stories from Radio and Television* (Oxford: Oxford University Press, 1992), 234.
9. Fred MacDonald, *Television and the Red Menace: The Video Road to Vietnam* (New York: Praeger, 1985), 195.
10. Mark Alvey, "'Too Many Kids and Old Ladies': Quality Demographics and 1960s U.S. Television," in *Television: The Critical View*, 7th ed., ed. Horace Newcomb (Oxford: Oxford University Press, 2007), 15–36. Previously published in *Screen* 45, no. 1 (2004).

11. "Color Set Owners Advertiser's Best Prospects" *Broadcasting*, June 21, 1965, 29.

12. Renata Adler, "Anyone for a Good Cry?" *New York Times*, March 31, 1968.

13. David Scott Diffrient, *M*A*S*H* (Detroit: Wayne State University Press, 2008), 10–11.

14. Jane Feuer, Paul Kerr, and Tise Vahigmagi, eds., *MTM "Quality Television"* (London: BFI, 1984), 56.

15. Paul Attallah, "The Unworthy Discourse: Situation Comedy in Television," in *Critiquing the Sitcom: A Reader*, ed. Joanne Morreale (Syracuse: Syracuse University Press, 2003), 91–115. First published in *Interpreting Television: Current Research Papers*, ed. Willard D. Rowland Jr. and Bruce Watkins (Beverly Hills: Sage, 1984).

16. Attallah, "Unworthy Discourse," 101–2.

17. Attallah, "Unworthy Discourse," 102.

18. See Kaja Silverman's *Male Subjectivity at the Margins* (New York: Routledge, 1992), especially chapter 2, "Historical Trauma and Male Subjectivity," 52–121.

Chapter 1

1. This is due in great part to the fact that it was shot in 1964, months before the network had made the decision on its color programming expansion.

2. Royce, *"Hogan's Heroes,"* 31.

3. "Laugh Track," *Wikipedia*, last modified January 18, 2011, http://en.wikipedia.org/wiki/Laugh_track#cite_ref-Kitman_1–1.

4. *Hogan's Heroes* has the standard division of airtime. The first three minutes are dedicated to an opening credit sequence and prologue. After a commercial, act 1 of the episode fills another ten to twelve minutes until the second break, followed by an eight- to ten-minute act 2 and commercial. After the third commercial break, the episode concludes with a one- to three-minute epilogue and thirty seconds of closing credits.

5. See Jaroslav Hasek's *The Good Soldier Schwejk and His Fortunes in the World War* (New York: Penguin Classics, 2005).

6. Royce, *"Hogan's Heroes,"* 131.

7. Royce, *"Hogan's Heroes,"* 190.

8. In the pilot episode it is, for some reason, referred to as Camp 13. Beginning with the second episode, "Hold That Tiger," the German abbreviation for *Stammlager* is used.

9. The quickest way to locate a version of this assertion is under the Klemperer entry on the Internet Movie Database at www.imdb.com/name/nm0459252/bio.

10. Royce, *"Hogan's Heroes,"* 82.

11. Royce, *"Hogan's Heroes,"* 43.

12. For a full account of genre reading, see Tanya Modleski's *Loving with a Vengeance: Mass-Produced Fantasies for Women* (New York: Methuen, 1984).

13. See the full entry for Gene Reynolds at www.imdb.com/name/nm0721728/.

14. The episode draws on the 1956 film of the same name about an attempted fixed boxing match.

15. Derek Kompare, *Rerun Nation: How Repeats Invented American Television* (New York: Routledge, 2005), 71.

16. Kompare, *Rerun Nation,* 71.

17. Long after the network run of *Hogan's Heroes*, President Reagan came under intense criticism for his visit to the cemetery of former SS officers in Bitburg, Germany. Critics argued that honoring them as fallen victims of war rendered them as unwilling victims of National Socialism rather than primary perpetrators of the regime's crimes.

18. Max Horkheimer and T. W. Adorno, *Dialectic of Enlightenment* (New York: Continuum, 1987), 138.

Chapter 2

1. See Royce, *"Hogan's Heroes,"* 17–21.

2. *New York Times*, September 18, 1965.

3. *New York Times*, October 17, 1965.

4. Jeffrey Shandler, *While America Watches: Televising the Holocaust* (New York: Oxford University Press, 1999), 84.

5. *New York Times*, April 16, 1978.

6. *New York Times*, April 20, 1978.

7. It is worth noting that no critiques came forward in the *New York Times* with such a detailed analysis of the juxtaposition of story detail and advertising in *Roots*. It is not hard to imagine similar absurdities arising there.

8. British, German, and other public television systems often work on a different model. For example, the BBC production *Rome*, which was syndicated in the United States by HBO, offered twenty-two episodes over two seasons. The story arc was designed from the start to span from the rise of Julius Caesar to the downfall of Mark Anthony

(though the producers did intend to extend the history into reign of Augustus before the set at Cinecittá was destroyed by fire). Nevertheless, this limited format is often used in a variety of genres on the BBC.

9. There have been three successful American historical sitcoms since the premiere of *M*A*S*H*: *Happy Days* (1975–84), *Laverne and Shirley* (1976–83), and *That '70s Show* (1998–2006). If *Happy Days* and *Laverne and Shirley* use a soapy nostalgia of the 1950s to counterbalance the social transformations of the intervening decades, *That '70s Show* reads as a response to that backlash, offering a less innocent view of Wisconsin during the period in which the former shows aired.

10. Hal Humphrey, "Banner Sticks to Stars and Stripes," *Los Angeles Times*, September 28, 1965, C13.

11. Royce, *"Hogan's Heroes,"* 91.

12. Leon Askin, with C. Melvin Davidson, *Quietude and Quest: Protagonists and Antagonists in the Theatre, On and Offstage* (Riverside: Ariadne Press, 1989), 81.

13. Royce, *"Hogan's Heroes,"* 120.

14. See Askin, *Quietude and Quest*, 204.

15. Clary provides an account of his life in *From the Holocaust to "Hogan's Heroes": The Autobiography of Robert Clary* (Lanham, MD: Madison Books, 2001).

16. Humphrey, "Banner Sticks," C13.

17. Jeanine Basinger, *The World War II Combat Film: Anatomy of a Genre* (Middleton, CT: Wesleyan University Press, 2003), 27.

18. Karl Marx, "The Eighteenth Brumaire of Louis Bonaparte" in *The Marx-Engels Reader*, 2nd ed., ed. Robert C. Tucker (New York: Norton, 1978), 594.

19. The only comparable programming was the widespread American network coverage of the Adolf Eichmann trials in Jerusalem. For a thorough discussion of those, see Shandler, *While America Watches*.

20. The famous Auschwitz trials in Frankfurt, which took place from 1963 to 1965, mark the Germans' first major postwar confrontation with the Holocaust. This also signals the beginning of a long and thorough confrontation with their own Nazi past, known in German as *Vergangenheitsbewältigung*. For an account of postwar German historical debates see Charles S. Maier, *The Unmasterable Past: History, the Holocaust, and National Identity* (Cambridge: Harvard University

Press, 1988) or my introduction to *Unwilling Germans: The Goldhagen Debate* (Minneapolis: University of Minnesota Press, 1998).

21. Basinger, *World War II*, 142.
22. See Royce, *"Hogan's Heroes,"* 23.
23. Royce, *"Hogan's Heroes,"* 22.

Chapter 3

1. Paul Buhle and David Wagner, *Hide in Plain Sight: The Hollywood Blacklistees in Film and Television, 1950–2002* (New York: Palgrave Macmillan, 2002), 62.
2. Jack Gould, "No Time for Situation Comedy," *New York Times*, December 17, 1967.
3. Gould, "No Time."
4. *New York Times*, April 12, 1966.
5. In 1969, *Hogan's Heroes* moved from its long-held position on Saturday night to the Friday night lineup.
6. Royce, *"Hogan's Heroes,"* 59.

FILMOGRAPHY

A Walk in the Sun (Lewis Milestone, 1945)

Alice (CBS, 1975–85)
All in the Family (CBS, 1971–79)
Andy Griffith Show, The (CBS, 1960–68)
Auto Focus (Paul Schrader, 2002)
Bataan (Tay Garnett, 1943)
Battleground (William A. Wellman, 1949)
Best Years of Our Lives, The (William Wyler, 1946)
Bob Newhart Show, The (CBS, 1972–78)
Burke's Law (ABC, 1963–66)
Campo 44 (NBC, 1967)
Catch 22 (Mike Nichols, 1970)
Combat! (ABC, 1962–67)
Convoy (NBC, 1965)
Diary of Anne Frank, The (George Stevens, 1959)
Dirty Dozen, The (Robert Aldrich, 1967)
Espionage (NBC, 1963–64)
F Troop (ABC, 1965–67)
Get Smart (NBC, 1965–69; CBS, 1969–70)
Gomer Pyle, U.S.M.C. (1964–69)
Grand Illusion, The (Jean Renoir, 1937)
Great Escape, The (John Sturges, 1963)

Hogan's Heroes

"The Informer" (September 17, 1965, dir. Robert Butler)

"The Flight of the Valkyrie" (October 15, 1965, dir. Gene Reynolds)

"The Gold Rush" (January 14, 1966, dir. Howard Morris)

"The Prince from the Phone Company" (March 18, 1966, dir. Gene Reynolds)

"The Safecracker Suite" (March 25, 1966, dir. Howard Morris)

"I Look Better in Basic Black" (April 1, 1966, dir. Howard Morris)

"Request Permission to Escape" (April 29, 1966, dir. Edward H. Feldman)

"The Rise and Fall of Sergeant Schultz" (October 21, 1966, dir. Gene Reynolds)

"A Tiger Hunt in Paris" (November 18 and 25, 1966, dir. Richard Powell)

"Don't Forget to Write" (December 9, 1966, dir. Gene Reynolds)

"The Swing Shift" (February 3, 1967, dir. Edward Feldman)

"The Tower" (March 17, 1967, dir. Gene Reynolds)

"Colonel Klink's Secret Weapon" (March 24, 1967, dir. Gene Reynolds)

"D-Day at Stalag 13" (September 23, 1967, dir. Gene Reynolds)

"Is General Hammerschlag Burning?" (November 18, 1967, dir. Edward Feldman)

"A Russian Is Coming" (November 25, 1967, dir. Bob Sweeney)

"The Hostage" (December 16, 1967, Edward Feldman)

"Two Nazis for the Price of One" (December 30, 1967, dir. Bruce Bilson)

"Hogan, Go Home" (January 13, 1968, dir. Edward H. Feldman)

"War Takes a Holiday" (January 27, 1968, dir. Bruce Bilson)

"Clearance Sale at the Black Market" (September 28, 1968, Edward Feldman)

"Will the Blue Baron Strike Again" (December 14, 1968, dir. Marc Daniels)

"The Softer They Fall" (January 23, 1970, dir. Richard Kinon)

"The Sergeant's Analyst" (March 6, 1970, dir. Bruce Bilson)

"Cuisine à la Stalag 13" (September 20, 1970, dir. Jerry London)

"To Russia without Love" (January 31, 1971)

"Rockets or Romance" (March 7, 1971)

Holocaust (NBC, 1978)

I Spy (NBC, 1965–68)

Inglorious Bastards (*Quel maledetto treno blindato*; Enzo Castellari, 1978)

Inglourious Basterds (Quentin Tarantino, 2009)

Jacob the Liar (Peter Kassovitz, 1999)
Jakob der Lügner (Frank Beyer, 1975)
Kelly's Heroes (Brian Hutton, 1970)
Life Is Beautiful (*La vita é bella*;Roberto Benigni, 1997)
Little Rascals
Longest Day, The (Ken Annakin, 1962)
Looney Tunes
Lou Grant (CBS, 1977–82)
Love, American Style (ABC, 1969–74)
Magnum P.I. (CBS, 1980–88)
Man from U.N.C.L.E., The (NBC, 1964–68)
Mary Tyler Moore Show, The (CBS, 1970–77)
M*A*S*H (CBS 1972–83)
McHale's Navy (ABC, 1962–66)
McKeever and the Colonel (NBC, 1962–63)
Mission: Impossible (CBS, 1966–73)
Mister Ed (CBS, 1961–66)
My Favorite Martian (CBS, 1963)
My Living Doll (CBS, 1964),
My Three Sons (CBS, 1960–72)
New Faces of 1952
Pawnbroker, The (Sidney Lumet, 1964)
Petticoat Junction (1963–70)
Phil Silvers Show, The (CBS, 1955–59)
Play Dirty (André De Toth, 1968)
Popeye
Roots (ABC, 1977)
Rowan and Martin's Laugh-In (NBC, 1967–73)
Sergeant York (Howard Hawks, 1940)
Smothers Brothers Comedy Hour, The (CBS, 1967–70)
Stalag 17 (Billy Wilder, 1954)
Story of G.I. Joe, The (William A. Wellman, 1945)
To Be or Not to Be (Ernst Lubitsch, 1942)
Twelve O'Clock High (1964–67)
Von Ryan's Express (Mark Robson, 1965)
Wackiest Ship in the Army, The (NBC, 1965–66)
Wake Island (John Farrow, 1942)
War and Remembrance (ABC, 1988; dir. Dan Curtis)
Wicked Dreams of Paula Schultz, The (George Marshall, 1968)

Wild One, The (Lazlo Benedek, 1953)
Winds of War (ABC, 1983; dir. Dan Curtis)
WKRP in Cincinnati (ABC, 1978–82)

115

Adorno, Theodor W., 7, 53
Alice, 60
All in the Family, 5, 104
American Broadcasting Company
    (ABC), 8, 14, 48, 51
Andy Griffith Show, The, 8, 104
Arsenic and Old Lace, 55
Askin, Leon, 26, 53–54, 64, 69, 72,
    79, 85
Auto Focus, 73

Banner, John, 2, 24, 53–56, 64, 69,
    72–73
barnyard purge, 12–13, 15
Basinger, Jeanine, 60, 68
Bataan, 68
Battleground, 68
Best Years of Our Lives, The, 68
Beverly Hillbillies, The, 12
Bob Newhart Show, The, 5
Brecht, Bertolt, 53

Campo 44, 11, 47
Catch 22, 71–72
civil rights, 34, 86

Clary, Robert, 21–22, 26, 54–56
Cold War, 8, 11, 33, 67, 72, 74, 78,
    87–88, 90, 92–93, 103
Columbia Broadcasting System
    (CBS), 1–14, 19, 25, 60, 76, 94,
    100
combat film, 20, 60, 63–64, 68–69,
    71–72
Combat!, 8, 48–49
concentration camp, 48, 50, 54,
    56, 64
Crane, Robert, 2, 22, 25, 72–73
Cronkite, Walter, 4, 76, 94, 96
cumulative narrative, 6

Dawson, Richard, 21–22, 26
Diary of Anne Frank, The, 50
Dirty Dozen, The, 71–73
Dixon, Ivan, 21–22, 25, 33, 40, 100

F Troop, 8, 63
Feldman, Edward H., 40, 77

Get Smart, 8, 80
Gilligan's Island, 104

Gomer Pyle, U.S.M.C., 8, 10–12, 14, 63, 80
Grand Illusion, The, 20
Great Escape, The, 69
Green Acres, 12

Happy Days, 122n9
Hee Haw, 12
Hilberg, Raul, 49
historical comedy, 52, 55
Hochman's Heroes, 48
Holocaust (TV miniseries), 51–52, 66–67
Holocaust, 47, 49–52, 64, 66–67, 74, 103
Horkheimer, Max, 7, 45, 53

I Spy, 8, 25, 80
Inglorious Bastards, 72
Inglorious Basterds, 72–73

Jakob the Liar, 50

Kelly's Heroes, 71–72
Kinsky, Leonid, 22, 55–56, 60, 88
Klemperer, Otto, 53
Klemperer, Werner, 2, 23, 28, 53, 64

Laverne and Shirley, 122n9
Life Is Beautiful, 50
Little Rascals, The, 42
Longest Day, The, 49, 59, 69–70
Looney Tunes, 42–43, 45
Lou Grant, 35
Lynde, Paul, 54

Magnum P.I., 6
Man from U.N.C.L.E., The, 8, 10–11, 25, 80, 86
Mann, Thomas, 53

Marx, Karl, 61
Mary Tyler Moore Show, The, 5, 35, 60
M*A*S*H, 2, 4–5, 14–15, 34, 52, 104
Mayberry R.F.D., 12
McHale's Navy, 8, 12, 14, 49, 63
McKeever and the Colonel, 14
military comedy, 2, 14, 47–48, 79–80, 93
Minow, Newton, 7
Mission: Impossible, 8, 25
MTM Enterprises, 13, 15

National Broadcasting Company (NBC), 8, 10–12, 14, 25, 47, 51, 86
Norman Lear, 13

Pawnbroker, The, 50
Petticoat Junction, 12, 86
Phil Silvers Show, The, 9–10
Pickelhaube, 61–62
Play Dirty, 71
Popeye, 42

quality television, 15, 104

race relations, 33, 38–40
Reagan, Ronald, 121n17
Reinhardt, Max, 54
Reynolds, Gene, 34
Rome, 121n8
Roots, 51–52
Ruman, Sig, 69

Schoenberg, Arnold, 53
Sergeant Bilko, 9
Sergeant York, 68
Stalag 17, 11, 20–21, 34, 64, 69
Story of G.I. Joe, The, 68

syndication, 3, 42, 44, 52, 64, 76, 100

Talbot, Nita, 88, 91
To Be or Not to Be, 69
Twelve O'Clock High, 8, 49

uniform comedy, 76. *See also* military comedy

vast wasteland, 7, 13
Vietnam, 3–5, 8–9, 11, 14–15, 36, 71, 74–76, 78, 82–83, 85, 87, 94, 97, 101, 103–4

Von Ryan's Express, 70

Wackiest Ship in the Army, The, 8
Wake Island, 68
Walk in the Sun, A, 68
War and Remembrance, 66
war film, 68
Wicked Dreams of Paula Schultz, The, 72
Wild One, The, 81
Winds of War, 66
WKRP in Cincinnati, 60
World War I, 24, 61–63, 68